To Autumn:

With love from your KeyBank friends,
you will be missed. Hope this
book is a blessing to you.

Brigitte
Vivian
Cristin

Friends
Through Thick & Thin

Friends Through Thick and Thin is a Women of Faith book.

Women of Faith is partnering with Zondervan Publishing House, Integrity Music, *Today's Christian Woman* magazine, and Campus Crusade to offer conferences, publications, worship music, and inspirational gifts that support and encourage today's Christian women.

Since their beginning in January of 1996, the Women of Faith conferences have enjoyed an enthusiastic welcome by women across the country. Women of Faith conference plans presently extend through the year 2000.

Call 1-888-49-FAITH for the many conference locations and dates available.

www.women-of-faith.com

Other Women of Faith Books for You to Enjoy

Joy Breaks
The Joyful Journey, book and audio
Bring Back the Joy, book and audio (available April 1998)

Friends
Through Thick & Thin

GLORIA GAITHER

PEGGY BENSON

SUE BUCHANAN

JOY MACKENZIE

ZondervanPublishingHouse

Grand Rapids, Michigan

A Division of HarperCollinsPublishers

Friends Through Thick and Thin
Copyright © 1998 by Gloria Gaither, Sue Buchanan, Peggy Benson, Joy MacKenzie

Requests for information should be addressed to:

ZondervanPublishingHouse
Grand Rapids, Michigan 49530

Library of Congress Cataloging-in-Publication Data

Friends through thick and thin / Gloria Gaither ... [et al.].
   ISBN: 0-310-21726-1 (hardcover)
     p.   cm.
   1. Women—psychology. 2. Female friendship. 3. Friendship—religious aspects—Christianity. I. Gaither,
Gloria.
HQ1206.F734 1998
302.3'4'082—dc21
                                     97-40900
                                        CIP

This edition printed on acid-free paper and meets the American National Standards Institute Z39.48 standard.

All Scripture quotations, unless otherwise indicated, are taken from the *Holy Bible: New International Version®*. NIV®. Copyright © 1973, 1978, 1984 by International Bible Society. Used by permission of Zondervan Publishing House. All rights reserved.

Scripture quotations marked (KJV) are from the Holy Bible, King James Version.

Scripture quotations marked (TLB) are taken from *The Living Bible* © 1971. Used by permission of Tyndale House Publishers, Inc., Wheaton, IL 60189. All rights reserved.

Scripture quotations marked (THE MESSAGE) are from *The Message: New Testament with Psalms and Proverbs*. Copyright © 1993, 1994, 1995 by Eugene H. Peterson. All rights reserved. Used by permission of NavPress Publishing Group.

"Old Friends." Words by Gloria Gaither. Music by William J. Gaither and J. D. Miller. © 1992 by Gaither Music Company, Life Gate Music, and Always Alive Music. All rights reserved. Used by permission.

Excerpts from the works of Bob Benson. © 1994 by Peggy J. Benson. All rights reserved. Used by permission.

"One Day Nearer Home." Words and music by Stuart Hamblen. © 1961, renewed 1989 Hamblen Music. All rights reserved. Used by permission.

"Invitation to a Feast" from *The Inspirational Writings of C. S. Lewis: The Four Loves.* © 1960 by Helen Joy Lewis. Used by permission.

"Metamorphosis" by Gloria Gaither. © 1974 by Gloria Gaither. All rights reserved. Used by permission.

"Elizabeth." Excerpts from the works of Bob Benson. © 1994 by Peggy J. Benson. All rights reserved. Used by permission.

"A Nun's Prayer." From *Little Book of Prayers.* © 1960 by Pauper Press. Used by permission.

"Is This All" by Dorothy Sickal. © by Dorothy Sickal. All rights reserved. Used by permission.

"Consider the Lillies." Words and music by Anne Ward Herring. © 1985 Birdwing Music. All rights reserved. Used by permission.

"When Love Gives." Words by Sue Buchanan and Steve Chapman. Music by Steve Chapman. © 1994 by Sue Buchanan and Times and Seasons Music. Used by permission.

"So I Won't Forget." Written by Gloria Gaither, from her journal, January 4, 1986. © 1988 by Gloria Gaither. All rights reserved. Used by permission.

Letters to a Young Poet by Rainer Mario Rilke, translated by Stephen Mitchell. Copyright © 1984 by Stephen Mitchell. Reprinted by permission of Random House, Inc.

"Friends in the Pew." From *Listening for a God Who Whispers* by Peggy Benson. © 1994 by Peggy J. Benson. All rights reserved. Used by permission.

"Count on Me." Words by Suzanne Jennings. Music by William J. Gaither, Guy Penrod, Woody Wright, and David Huntsinger. © 1996 Townsend and Warbucks Music, Gaither Music Company, Saddlebred Music, Our Town Music, and Huntsinger Music. All rights reserved. Used by permission.

"Friendship." Written by Gloria Gaither. © 1974 by Gloria Gaither. All rights reserved. Used by permission.

"Thank God for the Promise of Spring." Words and music by William J. and Gloria Gaither. © 1973 William J. Gaither. All rights reserved. Used by permission.

Published in association with the literary agency of Alive Communications, Inc., 1465 Kelly Johnson Blvd., #320, Colorado Springs, CO 80920.

Illustrations by Laura Leigh Benson-Greer
Interior design by Sue Vandenberg Koppenol

Printed in the United States of America

98 99 00 01 02 03 04 /❖ DC/ 10 9 8 7 6 5 4 3 2 1

To our husbands and children,
who have alternately encouraged, endured,
exaggerated, enjoyed, and occasionally editorialized
our efforts to tell this story of friendship.

Contents

Autumn's Quiet
... Friendship Savored

Winter's Promise
... Friends in Peril and Pleasure

A Word from Our Daughters

When I was a child, I thought friendship was about having fun: talk and laughter-filled sleepovers and long days at the pool. There was no way for me to know how much more friendship would mean to me as I grew older. I began to realize it the day we buried my father. Three hours before the funeral, my friend Brenda, whom I had not seen in two years, came to my door and almost literally physically supported me through the worst day of my life.

As a little girl, I loved listening to the conversations of my mother and her friends Joy, Sue, and Gloria. They were filled with laughter over things I did not remotely understand but found funny because they were so tickled over them.

Sue always fascinated me. She seemed flamboyant and exciting because she was wide *open!* She was the one person on earth that made my mother seem even remotely introverted. Sue has a great big personality, and I have a rather tiny one that I prefer to keep hidden. There were times when I feared her attention and the possibility of outlandish questions directed at me from across a crowded room. But I very clearly remember spilling a tray of drinks on her white carpet during a party and the gentle and quiet way in which she handled it so that I would not be humiliated.

Going to Joy's house was an adventure. I remember thinking that she actually glowed in the light, so sunny is her disposition. Her furnishings seemed exotic to me. Actually, she was just from the North, not the Polynesian Islands, but her house was filled with contemporary things, much different from the antique-filled rooms of my relatives. Most impressive to me were the brightly colored paintings and prints that I couldn't make head nor tail of and the huge, stuffed pillows you could lie around on any time you wanted. Joy was great with children. At her house, I was always treated as importantly as any adult visitor.

What I remember most about Gloria is how calm she always seemed to be. Even with kids running in and out, and guests and business (and Bill!) to see after, she remained totally unflustered. One time my friend Brenda and I were riding in the backseat of the Gaithers' car on a winding, country road. All of a sudden, there was a big thud.

"G-G-Gloria," stammered Bill in astonishment, "did we just hit a cow?"

"Yes, Bill, we did," said Gloria in a voice as calm as if she were ordering a hamburger!

I could not write about this group without saying some things about my mother who is, *not* incidentally, one of my best friends. Mom's love of people is more than just a passing curiosity about the stories of their lives. She has genuine compassion and concern for those she meets. Their faces, their stories, and most of their names are written forever on her heart. She smiles as she thinks of the fun she has shared with them and tears up as she remembers one of them in pain. Anyone who has met my mom even once has been in her thoughts or her prayers at one time or another, and as her many, many friends and relatives can tell you, that is a very special place to be.

These are four strong women. There is a lot more going on in their friendships than shopping, talking on the phone, or comparing notes about kids. These are women whose vulnerability and intimacy with each other bind them together in ways that make each of them stronger. When the painful times come, as they certainly do, they are able to give one another the strength to endure.

Recently a doctor asked me what I do for myself to stay well. I mentally searched through the list in my mind. Reading, perhaps? No. Nowadays I can read for only a few minutes without falling asleep. Exercise? Does driving by the YMCA several times a week count? Dates with husband, Tommy? Even if you can work around the ever-changing Little League schedule, where can you find an affordable, trustworthy sitter? Scrambling for an answer, I finally said, "Friends." Immediately, I knew it was the right answer. I go to my friends for light and humor, advice and renewal, a soaking for my soul, and sometimes, a good pruning. They are as necessary to me as oxygen and water.

So I see them differently now: Gloria and Joy and Sue and Mom. Although invisible to me as a child, their connectedness remained through disputes between husbands and crashed dreams. Through cancer and loss and fear for their children. As I look at them today,

I can see the shape of a friendship whose bonds tie them together and give them strength, making each of them more complete.

Leigh Benson-Greer

I don't think I can remember a time in the history of the Gaither family when the names Buchanan, MacKenzie, and Benson were not mentioned in conversation around our house at least once a day, usually in connection with some creative effort, album project, or live production. I remember waiting impatiently at the dinner table for my father, who was engrossed in some deep philosophical debate on the telephone with Bob MacKenzie. My mother would plead, "Bill, the food's getting cold," and because there was never any clever way to conclude these involved and infrequent dialogues, Dad would finally say, "You bet, buddy. Good-bye," and hang up.

I remember the vacations our families took together, the Bensons introducing us to Nantucket, Joy's discussions about elementary education, Peggy's southern accent and clever one-liners, Wayne's hearty laugh, Bob MacKenzie's and Daddy's infamous moped wreck in Cayman, Sue's crazy practical jokes and helpful photography tips, Bob's softly spoken stories.

And I remember thinking that I was fortunate that my parents' friends, in addition to being educated, handsome, and humorous, were really "cool." "Cool," as I eventually came to realize, meant that, although they were all evangelical Christians, serious Bible scholars, and faithful churchgoers, they were always open to new ideas, no matter how far-out or far-fetched. They loved any discourse on issues, and they never let any idea—even time-honored traditions handed down from beloved parents—go untested. Because of my early associations with these interesting characters, I developed an incredible confidence in my abilities and opinions, and I knew that any supposition, however underdeveloped, that came from my adolescent brain had, at least, the right to be entertained.

With the passage of time, I realize how dissimilar, yet how alike these individuals were and are, and I am amazed and also not amazed that the bonds of friendship have remained so strong over the years—in spite of diversity, life experiences, separation, and death. Theirs is a union that has taught me a lesson about comradeship; that a patron, an advocate, a colleague, an ally, a cohort is one who has made a covenant to another by esteem, respect, and affection; that a true friend "sticks closer than a brother." I realize, especially now that I am in my thirties, trying to raise a family in this extremely disjointed society, the importance of developing and cultivating friendships that are lasting.

So, thank you, ladies, for your insight, your advice, your example, but most of all . . . thank you for being friends.

Suzanne Gaither Jennings

As a child, I spent many hours peering out from beneath a restaurant tablecloth, a giant beach umbrella, or a department store clothing rack at my mother and her friends. I recognized them for the simple things that only a four-year-old could appreciate—the exotic colors of Sue's eye shadow, Gloria's crayon-laden tote bag, Peggy's ever-present cup of coffee, and the clean lotioned smell of my mother's skin as she lifted me up for a kiss. At this stage, I never considered the lifelong impact these women would have on a curly-haired, inquisitive little girl.

As a teenager, I watched them warily from the safe harbor of my bedroom. They were most often in the kitchen, congregated around various forms of chocolate delectables. I learned early that these women were unpredictable. They were capable of shenanigans that could strike fear into the heart of an awkward junior-higher. They might show up unannounced at school, sing too loudly at church, or worse—tell baby stories to your friends whom you wanted so desperately to think you were cool. These women were loud intruders in the life of a perpetually embarrassed fourteen-year-old.

Now, as an adult, I study them intently, wondering what secrets they trade as they float in and out of each other's lives. I attempt to listen to the stories they tell as they crowd on the bed for a late-night discussion. I strain to hear their laughter as it wafts through the house. I cannot get enough of their interactions for the simple reason that they delight and revitalize my spirit. I am drawn to their company, their wit, their exchange of ideas, their language.

These women all possess the gift of exuberant conversation, although at times, I know their children and husbands would trade it for the gift of silence. When I need an opinion, a prayer, or a dose of mothering, it is readily available in quantities that will last me through the next several challenges. Their presence is now vital and constant in my life. It is a model for how friends should be—loving, forgiving, and full of celebration. I find myself rearranging my schedule just to experience them. I would accept an invitation from them to a potluck dinner, a garden weeding, even to watch them paint each other's toenails! I love their company because I know there will always be nonstop, stimulating conversation, hilarity, celebration . . . and chocolate!

Shana Leigh MacKenzie

Since being asked to put in my two cents about my mother and her friends—I'm writing this long before the book is due to be published—I've been worrying about one thing: What do they intend to put on the cover? When I think about my mother and her friends, I certainly don't picture teacups, cabbage roses, and pink ribbons (the kind of thing you usually see on the cover of a "womansy" book like this one).

After all, theirs isn't your average, ask-no-questions, pass-no-criticism type of friendship. It isn't even an "If you can't say something nice about somebody, well then . . ." kind of friendship! Actually, I'm thinking sandpaper might be a better image for a book on friendship by Mama, Joy, Gloria, and Peggy!

What it is, from my perspective, is a friendship that refines. A friendship that challenges. A friendship that isn't afraid to speak its mind or take the big risk—even when it hurts.

As a young kid and a fly-on-the-wall observer of this foursome of women (and of course, the men in their lives—Daddy, Bob MacKenzie, Bill Gaither, and Bob Benson), I remember listening in on countless conversations that might be considered "risky" in the Christian circles I find myself in today. No subject was too sacred to be discussed, examined, analyzed, unraveled, and critiqued. No idea went uncontested. No theological mountain was too monumental to scale. They questioned each other's conclusions and offered innumerable theories and opinions.

Sometimes it got personal. "That lyric you wrote could have been stronger." "The concert last night wasn't bad, but nobody hit the ball out of the park." "I think you need to work a little harder on your writing" (or your music, or your grammar, or your worldview—you get the picture!). Excellence was a big thing with these people—and nobody got by with a subpar performance.

I didn't know it at the time, but Proverbs 27:18 describes this type of synergism in relationships: "As iron sharpens iron, so one man [or woman] sharpens another." Of course, from my vantage point as a daughter, this sharpening process didn't always seem like a good thing. As a teenager I remember thinking about my parents' friends (they were my friends too) and wondering, "Wouldn't it be better to have friends who accepted you unconditionally, embraced your ideas uncritically, allowed your goals and ideas to remain unchallenged, who just let you be average, for heaven's sake?"

Maybe for some people. But it was too late for me. I was ruined for the ordinary, unexamined life by eight people who have gone the distance with each other and with me—two parents, and six parents-through-friendship, who often played the role of parents when, for various reasons, my own didn't do the trick. And though they've sometimes been my strongest critics, they've also been my most enthusiastic cheerleaders. I suppose by now, and with the publishing of this book, they know that they too have a cheerleader—in me!

Dana Buchanan Shafer

Old Friends

Old friends,
After all of these years, just old friends,
Through the laughter and tears, old friends,
What a find! What a priceless treasure!
Old friends, like a rare piece of gold—
Old friends make it great to grow old:
Til then, through it all I will hold to old friends.

Oh, God must have known
There'd be days on our own
We would lose our will to go on—
That's why He sent friends like you along—
Old friends, yes, you've always been there,
My old friends: we've had more than our share—
Old friends, I'm a rich millionaire in old friends.

A phone call, a letter, a pat on the back,
Or a "Hey, I just dropped by to say ..."
A hand when we're down,
A loan when we just couldn't pay:
A song or a story, a rose from the florist,
A note that you happened to send
Out of the blue just to tell us that you're still our friend ...

We've been through some tough times
When we didn't know whether we'd even have one thin dime—
But that didn't change you:
You stayed by our side the whole time:
And when we were big winners
And everything seemed to be finally going our way—
You just cheered us on, so glad to be able to say ...

Old friends, yes you've always been there,
Old friends, we've had more than our share—
Old friends, I'm a rich millionaire, in old friends.

Gloria Gaither

And Then There Were Four

Take one sweet, petite southern belle. Mix with one tall, leggy West Virginian; add two mischievous Michiganders. What do you have? An unlikely recipe for friendship!

The four of us are very different, but, like most people who enjoy a long-term relationship, we are also very much alike.

Peggy is a sort of southern Edith Bunker. She has the ability to be incredibly profound without even realizing it, yet she will leave you howling with laughter at some outrageous truth. She mothers the world. I guess she must have gotten into the habit when she had a husband who spent his life thinking, reading, and speaking and five kids who expected and received a great deal of care. I tell her she could have been a great thinker and speaker all those years, too—if she'd had a good wife!

Peggy can get away with things none of the rest of us can because she weighs only about one hundred pounds, soaking wet, and speaks with a slow, southern drawl that makes her seem innocent, or, at least, if not quite innocent, then charming and helpless. She's about as innocent and helpless as a man-o'-war mistaken for a jellyfish on the beach. We all know this and have for thirty years! Yet we keep finding ourselves taking care of her as if she's fragile. Those steel magnolias will fool you every time.

Joy, on the other hand, seems always self-sufficient, pulled together, and organized. In truth, she probably needs someone to take care of her, because everyone dumps responsibility on her and she's always overloaded. Yet she always seems to have things under control, including all of us! She gives instructions like the teacher she is, corrects our grammar, double-checks our reservations, and is always the chosen moderator if we speak as a foursome.

Joy and I share a very similar background—first as PKs (preacher's kids), then as educators and as survivors with our husbands in the music business. I know her well enough to know that there are days, in spite of her façade of efficiency, when she is really a not-so-confident girl who needs someone to notice when she is too weary to breathe and to protect her from her own "yeses."

Then there's Sue. Now, Sue's main ploy in life is to be the dumb blonde. She's about as dumb as Peggy is fragile and as Joy is self-sufficient. Under that guise of flirt and flamboyance is an amazingly savvy businesswoman who actually has been documented as a reader of real books! And I don't mean *Elvis Sightings at the Memphis Mall*. Sue's image as the one who will take a dare, wear the wildest outfits, start a conversation with a piranha, and catch every funny thing that happens in church, is accurate.

Having Sue for a friend is fun but risky. You never know what she's going to do. Or say. Or wear! She's been known to sit on the lap of a perfect stranger (to her, but not to you); put a flimsy negligee in your husband's suitcase when he's not looking, then howl with laughter when she walks in as you are questioning him about how it got there; or send you an embarrassing postcard in the mail through your local everybody-there-knows-me, small-town post office.

Over the years, Sue and I have often been mistaken for one another. This amazes me, since I have always been famously flat-chested and Sue's main physical feature has been her enviable bust-line. (You should have seen her before reconstructive surgery!) Nonetheless, whenever Sue has been at one of our concerts, invariably someone has asked her to autograph a recording or book. I know this because I have seen people hand Bill a recording to sign that already has my autograph, but not in my handwriting. I shudder to think what Sue said to those trusting folks while they were thinking she was I. I am sure she had great fun making up stories or asking them questions. My reputation has probably taken many a hit on those occasions. On others, I've been mistaken for her, and it was her reputation that suffered a setback.

These three are outrageously different perennials in my garden of friends. We came together when life had set a deep plow in the soil of our hearts and we were ready for the seeds of friendship to germinate.

It was Peggy and Bob who brought us all together. Bob had joined his father at the Benson Publishing Company, a music business started by Bob's grandfather, John T. Benson Sr., to print gospel songbooks. By the time Bob became president, this humble company had grown to be one of the five or six major independent Christian music publishing and recording entities in the world.

Bob and Peggy were busy, not only working with songwriters and recording artists but raising a family of five children of their own. Bob had heard the Gaither Trio (at that time made up of my husband, his brother Danny, and his sister Mary Ann) sing, probably at a Nazarene camp meeting, since both Bill and Bob were from that same church background. Bill and I had not been married long but were by then writing songs together.

Bob talked to Bill about maybe recording an album and mentioned a new young producer the Benson company had recently hired. "I'd like you and Gloria to meet Bob MacKenzie and talk to him about what you could do with your songs." Bob Benson explained that Bob MacKenzie had come to Nashville from the East Coast to be general manager of the Nashville Symphony. "Gloria, you're going to love his wife, Joy," he said.

So we met Joy and Bob MacKenzie. Joy looked a lot like the Swedish and Norwegian girls I had known in Michigan. "I'm from Michigan," Joy told me. In no time we discovered that we had spent our high school years ninety miles apart, in two Michigan towns of similar size (Clare and Petoskey), in two very similar homes with amazingly similar mothers and fathers. We had both attended Christian colleges, both majored in French and English, and had both taught high school. We loved literature and the thrill of playing with words on the page. Our first meeting was short; yet when we left each other, I felt I had found a soul sister.

The next summer Bob Benson called to say that he and Peggy had rented a cottage in Nantucket. "Why don't you bring the kids and come out for a week? Our family will be leaving on the weekend; then Bob and Joy MacKenzie will come while you're there, and you can get better acquainted."

Bill was still teaching high school English at the time, and we were singing on the weekends. Summer was family time and we decided an island vacation would be great fun. We asked my mother to go along to help with our three children, packed up the bathing suits, and headed to the East Coast.

Bob and Joy arrived at the cottage with their little girl, Shana, and a brand new baby, Kristen. Our seven-year-old Suzanne was sandwiched in age between the two youngest Benson boys, Tom and Patrick. Next came our four-year-old Amy, then Shana and Benjy who were both about three, and then baby Kristen. Leigh Benson was a much older, wiser twelve-year-old, who was used to mothering her brothers and immediately took on the others as well.

Joy's mother, Florence Titus, and my mother, Dorothy Sickal, were also part of the incredible crew that filled that cottage—three families in all.

The entertainment the children most remember was the morning ritual of bathing new baby, Kristen, in the kitchen sink after the breakfast dishes were put away. Tom and Patrick Benson; Suzanne, Amy, and Benjy Gaither; and Shana MacKenzie would all line up like little ducks in a row with their faces just barely peeking over the edge of the sink, to watch this marvelous little creature being carefully lowered into the water in what almost seemed to be a ceremonial baptism. The baby was a marvel! Her round face and tiny perfect body rippled with life as she responded to all the squeals of laughter and adoration.

It was Bob Benson who asked us all, including the children, to write in their vacation book, which they left when the Bensons departed for home. It was an empty book in which all who had visited the house recorded their vacation memories, insights, adventures, and observations. Some wrote poetry, others just a musing about the ocean or the food or the fellowship.

One of Bob Benson's entries read

> Tonight up at Brandt Point the tide was way out and Tom and Pak (Patrick) and I were walking around the beach by the Coast Guard Station. Tom said when he got bigger he was going to join the Coast Guard—and it did look fun with their boats and dormitories. Then he said, "You'll be living then, won't you, Dad—I mean if you don't have a heart attack or something like that—won't you?" I said I would if nothing happens—and he squeezed my hand for a second and said—"Stay healthy, Dad, stay healthy—"

Little did we know then that Bob was beginning a fourteen-year struggle with cancer that would eventually leave Peggy the first widow among us.

From that week on, our families have been forever bonded. We went on to start companies such as Paragon, Ariose, Impact, and Gaither Music; realize shared dreams like Praise Gathering for Believers, the Lake Barkley Artist Retreat, and Family Fest in the Smokies; and to create a number of projects such as the musicals *Alleluia* and *Kids Under Construction*, the hymnal, *Hymns for the Family of God*, and many Gaither Trio recordings. We have succeeded and failed. Together and apart. Yet it has been our friendship that has remained important through it all.

Not long after the Nantucket week, we met another couple who were new at the Benson Company, Wayne and Sue Buchanan. They had two little girls, Dana and Mindy, who were about the ages of our Suzanne and Amy.

"Just wait till you meet Sue!" someone would always say, as if meeting Sue was some sort of initiation rite. Bill and I were soon introduced to Sue and Wayne at a Benson reception. Sue was a tall, sexy blonde and Wayne a friendly easy man whom we seemed to have always known. We soon learned that he was from Indiana, and he and Bill began to exchange stories and recollections of basketball games and growing up on a Hoosier farm. Sue and I talked about our kids and about the music business and our songs, but we really didn't get to know each other well until Bill came home one day and said, "Sue and Wayne are coming up for a day or so."

I'll never forget their arrival. I invited them into our family room and went to get coffee and refreshments. Our little two-year-old son just stood there looking at Sue and then followed her into the family room. I am sure he had never seen anyone with a bustline quite like Sue's! With her tall, blonde good looks, he was totally enamored. Before I could intervene, he climbed up in her lap and started poking her chest as if he were honking a horn. "Toot! Toot!" he said. I was mortified. Sue only laughed and Wayne chuckled as he said, "That's okay. He's not the first one to do that!"

After a beginning like that, there weren't many barriers left, and we became easy friends. We've laughed a lot together over the years. As it has turned out, we've cried a bit together, too.

We have traded children and shared our deep longings. We have sent notes and faxes and exchanged groanings that could not be uttered in prayer. Sue has always kept us laughing; sometimes we laughed because there were no more tears.

Her girls have been like my own children. When Dana was in college at Anderson University, the phone would ring sometimes on Sunday afternoon. I'd pick up the receiver and a small voice would say, "Whatcha doing?" "Oh, not much; just taking naps and making grilled cheese sandwiches. Want me to come get you?" I'd jump in the car and go get Dana at the dorm. She'd snuggle into some corner of our house and study or hang out by the kitchen fire, and we'd talk over a cup of hot chocolate. It felt good and natural to have her.

When Benjy was working in Nashville at Star Song and he was lonely and homesick, Wayne would call him and say, "Hey, man! You wanna go get some lunch tomorrow?" And our son would find a dad away from home.

When our daughter Amy was a student at Vanderbilt, she would often call Peggy or Joy or Sue and say, "I'm homesick; can I come over for supper?" She'd call me with the sound of her old self in her voice and I'd know my friends had enfolded our daughter into the embrace of their home when my arms couldn't reach her.

Over the years there have been many more shared vacations and interfamily adventures. We have remained friends through wrinkles and bulges, successes and failures, triumphs and disappointments. We have been a peer group who held each other accountable to be faithful to our marriage vows, to our God-given abilities, to our commitments to parenthood, and to our own personal integrity. Yet we have all felt from each other mercy, forgiveness, and love.

The seasons have come and gone. None of us even remember our original hair color, nor do we want to know what it might be now. We have changed shapes and sizes many times. We have loved each other through babies, businesses, and bunions. We have survived career changes, corporate collapses, and cancer. The ties that bind us have so many strands that we could never unwind them. They have been entwined by the hand of God, who has carefully woven the threads of our lives into a strong lifeline to Himself. This is the bond we share that has held through all the changing seasons of our lives. As a mutual friend, Stuart Hamblen, once wrote in a song we used to sing:

Each day is a measure on life's little string;
When reaching its ending tired eyes will behold
The string tied to the door latch of our Father's house.
One day nearer home—

Tender Spring

...A Time
for Beginnings

Gardening Thoughts

When the four of us began to talk about a book, the big question seemed to be how we would tie our ideas together. Joy, the English teacher, suggested we use a metaphor.

"How about gardening?" enthused Peggy, catching the spirit.

"Love it!" responded Gloria.

"Gardening it is!" the three of them shouted in unison.

"How about railroad?" I muttered. "You guys sure railroaded that one through." I was talking to myself. They were ignoring me.

"We can talk about the *seasons* of friendship. The *seeds* of friendship. The *blossoms* of friendship. The blah! blah! blah! . . . of friendship!" On and on they went.

"What shall we call this book?" I asked. *Bloom Where You're Planted?* It's been done. *Everyday bloomers?* Sounds like underwear. *Bloomin' idiots?* Banish the thought!

The truth is, Peggy is the only honest-to-goodness gardener in the bunch. She loves to work in the garden—really gets into it! Just the other day she told me she had planted Johnny-jump-ups. "Now I'm worried the inchworms will get them," she said. "Those inchworms are mean! They'll eat the pretty little faces right off those flowers if you don't watch them." (Watch them? Do you sit there all night with a shotgun waiting to blow the inchworms to smithereens? Wouldn't that take out the flowers as well?) It's a true gardener who worries about her Johnny-jump-ups to that extent!

Gloria is a gardener by principle. I'm sure she loves the *idea* of a garden, but I doubt it's something she sits around and worries about. "Okay, tomorrow I'll move the tall blue flowers over behind the little dumpy yellow ones and add some green fern-looking stuff. And let's see, maybe I'll spread some manure on the strawberries while I'm at it." (Gee! I put cream and sugar on my strawberries, but what do I know?)

I must say, Gloria has the big picture when it comes to the environment and cares about it very deeply, but if she has a Martha Stewart calendar that tells you when to mulch, I haven't seen it.

Joy couldn't care less about gardening. She liked the gardening concept because she liked the thought of using a metaphor—being an English teacher and all. One day Peggy and I were floating on mats in Joy's pool and were noticing how beautiful her flowers were—how picture perfect and how they had kept their bloom all summer in spite of the intense heat. When we took a closer look we discovered every single pot was full of—are you ready for this?—silk flowers! *Silk flowers!* Not only that, but when we questioned her about our discovery, Joy told us she bought them at the *funeral home outlet* because "the ones you put on graves last longer than the others." I ask you, is this a gardener?

My thumb isn't green. Never has been. Never will be. Gardening is not my thing. At least I admit it. In my opinion, you do gardening just as you do laundry and grocery shopping. It's not a career choice. Besides, I pay big bucks for these fingernails. Do I want dirt under them? I don't think so. And have you ever smelled compost? Do you even know what compost is?

If you sense, as you read this book, that I haven't caught the spirit of the metaphor and that I haven't fully cooperated, you, dear reader, are very perceptive! Another thing! What's a metaphor? Where I come from, it's a place to keep your cows!

Preparing the Soil of Friendship

A friendship starts long before two people are seen chatting comfortably over a cup of coffee, just as a garden begins long before an array of brightly colored blossoms sway lazily in the summer breeze.

Before anything can be planted, the soil must be ready. The hardened, impacted clods of winter must be broken apart and softened. Bad experiences, injury, and pain from the past may leave hearts too tough and scarred, too immovable, too judgmental and suspicious to accept the seeds of friendship.

Often, we must allow the softening mulch of God's forgiveness to give air and breath to the soil of our hearts. Prejudices—taught in our childhood or imposed by our society—must be released. Fear must be replaced by trust, and suspicion by childlike hope and acceptance. These changes in the soil will not come easily or without sweat, but any good gardener knows that preparing the soil is the most important of all labors. It gives the seeds a chance to grow and, eventually, to exhibit all that is hidden in its complex genetic structure.

Winter Dreams

Peggy

Tucked away in a corner of the condominium complex where I live is a tiny plot of land I call my garden. Though it's small, it's large enough to keep me interested in its well-being. On a cold winter morning in February, I sit at the breakfast room table, sipping my coffee, and stare through the gray, gloomy winter day to a dream of warm spring days and cool nights. Books, catalogs, and sketches laid out before me, I am already making a plan for my garden.

Stretched out by the sidewalk, I can see what appear to be empty clumps of soil and mulch. A closer look reveals a scattering of dead-looking shoots. But I look again. At the base of each dead stem, where it meets the earth, I can see minute shoots of greenery waiting impatiently for that moment when the cold gray of winter gives way to the warm rains and bright sunshine of spring. The earth will begin to thaw. The temperature will rise and cause the small plants to brave the cool nights and poke their heads above the surface of the ground. Suddenly the design of my garden begins to take shape.

Almost overnight, shades of green—from the soft hues of maidenhair fern to the intense green of rosemary and sweet boxwood—pop up everywhere. Healthy perennials and clumps of tulips, daffodils, and hyacinths blow gently in the breeze. The yard rollicks in a riot of color! The intensity is breathtaking! Deciduous shrubs that have slept through the winter begin to bud. Then blossom. Then burst into a kaleidoscope of pastels. In the far end of the garden, the birds are busy talking to each other as they fly from bath to feeder and back again, splashing and fluttering, fluttering and splashing. They have good news. Spring is finally here!

I run to the door and throw it open, drink in the sights and sounds of spring, smell the freshly mown grass and the fragrance of the blossoms. I can resist no longer. I grab my scissors and spade, my garden basket and old straw hat, and rush to bury my hands in the good, rich, moist earth. After a long winter, it is good to quit dreaming and deal with reality.

The way I see it, gardening is an opportunity to assist God in one of His loveliest miracles. To nurture and care for His creation. My plot of land may be small, but it's enough to remind me, all year long—HE IS ALIVE!

I need friends the way I need to garden. I need the challenge of it—preparing the soil, working at the task. Blooms don't just happen, you know! I need the cultivation process—giving it time and attention, learning when to water, when to feed, and when to be patient.

Finally, I need to see the color of the garden—the rewards for a job well done. It's in the beauty and the bounty that we see the results of our efforts.

Lessons in a Goldfish Bowl

In my growing-up years, I never thought of my mother as my friend. In the 1940s and 50s, mothers were just mothers—they weren't supposed to be friends. But my mom was a maverick, and her relationship with her four children was anything but traditional. A busy preacher's wife and matriarch of the Baptist parsonage, her contributions to my father's ministry would, today, fit a composite description of Christian education director, coordinator of women's ministries, youth director, administrative assistant, and church secretary. Music was the only part of the life of the church in which she had no input— Mother was a monotone bass (no kidding) who could play only one song on the piano, and a fitting song it was: "Work for the Night Is Coming." The title spoke volumes about her life ethic.

In her "spare time" away from the family and the church, she still did some substitute teaching and continued her graduate courses. She was an insatiable learner, finally completing her master's degree at the age of fifty-five—the same summer I got mine. She had racked up sixty-some credit hours over the years. My degree represented the normal thirty-four!

If she was guilty of idolatry, words were her god. No one else's mom served poetry with breakfast. Half of our kitchen wall was a large, heavy slate blackboard on which she wrote choice snatches of Scripture and poetry that we four children were to memorize—before supper. Repetition being the law of learning in those days, she would chant and clap and overdramatize the lines with us until we were overcome, either by laughter or irascible impatience. Her solution to my boyfriend problems was, typically, to write the boys riddles or silly poems. Sometimes they contained a personal admonishment:

> Young love is an adventure
> Which is riddled with temptation,
> So this request I offer

For your serious contemplation:
Be circumspect, and try to keep
Your hands just where you oughter
Leave "discovery" to Columbus;
Feast your eyes upon my daughter!

Our irritation with a gnarly parishioner was often assuaged by making the offender the subject of a saucy cooperative effort at rhyme, which we chanted with relish and uncontrolled laughter.

Here lies Deacon Smith, so cold
His scowl fixed, dark and dour
The sight of children changed his air
From satisfied to sour.
Now relaxed and free of care,
He spends each happy day
Where preachers' children line the curbs
Of Heaven's golden way!

It was this unconventional, crazy lady who shaped my image of mother, ministry, and yes, friendship. Oh, I was unaware of the influence at the time. Only decades later, when I set out to define the qualities of friendship, did I realize the benefits of what I had learned in the parsonage!

Most preacher's kids hated their "fishbowl" existence. Gloria and I are possibly the only exceptions I know of, and I've no doubt that our mothers made all the difference. They made the challenge of parsonage life an adventure. Our small churches were like microcosms of Dickens' novels; the whole odd spectrum of humanity dwelt therein. We were allowed to react honestly and openly to the frustrations of being preacher's kids. Through the tears and laughter, we also learned to become positively involved in the lives of other people. The hurting, the hapless, the homeless seemed to gravitate to our front door. I rarely slept in my own room; more often than not, it was occupied by a vagrant or a missionary on furlough.

One day, as my high school boyfriend and I arrived home from school, Mother met us on the porch.

"Kids!" she blurted in desperation, "I have an Indian in the bathtub!" We dissolved into laughter at the familiar tone of dramatic urgency. As the story unfolded, we learned that the man, a Mohawk

Indian, had been walking five days in stormy weather, across the Straits of Mackinaw from Michigan's upper peninsula. A missionary had given him my father's name as a contact, should he need food or housing. He was cold and hungry, and his clothes were wet and soiled. What he seemed to need most was a bath, so Mom had attempted to wash his clothes while the man bathed, but they had disintegrated in the washing machine. Mom wanted us to go to the house of the missions chairman to find some suitable clothing. "Your father's clothes are too small," she said. "And hurry! The poor soul is probably shaking with the shivers!"

Daily life in the parsonage was a combination of chaotic exhilaration and serious challenge. Somehow, Mother made us feel that at the end of the bedlam, there was always a party to be enjoyed. We learned to value people and their peculiarities.

The lessons of friendship were deeply ingrained—discipline; patience; self-sacrifice; how to create fun out of frustration, persist with others through all kinds of trials, and ride over the storm, knowing that behind the clouds, the sun was always shining; accepting what is; enjoying the good times; persevering through the bad.

To my future benefit and delight, these were the early lessons of life that laid the foundation for a joyful succession of enduring relationships.

Learning to Trust a Friend

I was loved as a child. Adored. My parents did not spoil me with indulgences that were condescending. They genuinely liked me and made me feel I had something viable to contribute to them, to our family, and to the world. This word is not often applied to children, but I had the feeling my parents *admired* me. I was always able to talk to them about the things that mattered to me, and knew I would be taken seriously.

This relationship laid the groundwork for being able to trust other people. In general, I think I'm not a very suspicious person when it comes to friends. I feel safe in taking them at face value and believe what they tell me to be the truth as they see it. When I am betrayed—and I have been on rare occasions—I am always surprised. It's not what I expect. I tend to feel there must have been some mistake.

Friendship, like gardening is, at once, toil, sweat, tears, fears, anxious moments about the elements, disappointments at pestilence or loss, and exuberant celebration at the sensory pleasures of the harvest.

Wax Build-up, Anthropology, and Starched Pillowcases

The first time I remember making a conscious effort to cultivate friends was when Wayne and I were first married. We lived in a tiny fourth-floor walk-up apartment in an industrial suburb of Chicago. We commuted two hours a day to and from the city to our daytime jobs. To supplement our income, Wayne was music director, and I was his accompanist, in a small church.

Our apartment would be called delightful, even charming, by today's standards. That was before we learned to appreciate ancient buildings with hardwood floors, thick plaster walls, and fourteen-foot ceilings with triple-crown molding.

It never occurred to us to turn the ugly, black fire escape outside our kitchen window into a balcony of beauty by adding pots of pansies and geraniums, or into a ledge of usefulness with an herb garden of parsley and oregano.

We were anxious to make friends in those days. We often managed to pack the whole church choir into our three-room apartment for a party, and once in a great while, we could save enough money for an evening in the city with others from the young adult Sunday school class. These were times of raucous laughter and fun, but it wasn't the same as having close *couple* friends—people with whom we could savor a good meal and more importantly, enjoy lively conversation.

I'll never forget the first couple we entertained. The conversation never veered from one topic. *Cleaning.* Cleaning, as in cleaning our scroungy little apartments. "What did you guys do today?" I asked as we sat down to dinner. Since I asked the leading question, I suppose you could say it was my fault that, for the next three hours, we discussed such things as the cause of wax build-up and how to rid ourselves of this pesky blight. *Steel wool? Razor blades? Ajax? Bon-Ami? Or perhaps some miracle-working commercial product yet to be discovered.*

We pondered! *Why are there hairs all over our bathroom floors? So many hairs you would think a Siberian husky was in residence.* Again, every possibility was examined, and I'm embarrassed to say that with all four of our brains working full blast, we came up with no definitive, you-can-swear-by-it answer.

"Do you iron your sheets? Do you starch your pillowcases? Do you carry your garbage down to the alley every day or every other day?"

"Do you change your dishwater before you scour your pots and pans?" They did! And they said so vehemently! *And* they had some pretty disparaging remarks about people who didn't! When all eyes turned to me, I certainly wasn't going to admit to being one of *those* people.

"It's like adding grease to grease," I said. "I not only run fresh water—hot, hot water—I *double* the soap!" Now I'm not proud of this—because it was all a huge lie—but I then wrinkled up my nose, leaned across the table, and said in a voice barely above a whisper, that I couldn't *possibly* cook my next meal in pans with a grease residue as thick as the grease on Elvis's pompadour.

A few weeks later Wayne suggested we try again and invite another couple for dinner. We barely knew Ernie and Barb. They came to church only on special occasions, probably to please Ernie's parents who never missed a service. They sat reverently on the side next to the organ—Ernie's mother was the organist—with tolerant little smiles that made me think they knew something the rest of us didn't. In the words of Ernie's mother, they were both "smart as a crack, and working night and day on their doctors" (sic). Down deep I thought perhaps some of their "smart as a crack" would rub off on us and at the very least, the dinner conversation would be more stimulating than it was with Mr. and Mrs. Grease Residue.

On the appointed evening, I cooked a big pot of spaghetti, which was all we could afford at the time, and tossed a salad. Wayne sliced the French bread and adjusted the HiFi (before stereo). My Formica-topped table looked elegant in the candlelight, set perfectly with my new wedding china and crystal.

"Nice apartment," Ernie Jr. muttered as he looked around. "We could never invite friends over. We have books stacked everywhere. Every table. Every chair. Barely a path to the bathroom."

"Nice table," Barb commented. "China and crystal are such a bother. In fact, ours is stored, and it will be stored till we're out of graduate school. Perhaps longer. It'll be years before we have time to entertain." This last statement caused me to rule out the fact that we might receive a reciprocal invitation any time soon.

Within the first five minutes we learned that our guests were not taking the easy way out (they told us this) when it came to their education. Both were majoring in anthropology.

For the life of me I couldn't remember a thing about anthropology except for some lyrics to a Smothers Brothers song that said, "My old man's an anthropologist, now whattaya think about that? He wears an anthropologist raincoat and an anthropologist hat." I knew Wayne was thinking the same thing and I saw his mouth fly open in disbelief when, in my most polite voice, I asked, "Exactly what does an anthropologist do?" (I *knew!* I just couldn't recall at the moment.)

Their explanation flew over my head like a buzzard honing in on roadkill, and it was downhill from there. Just as with couple number one, my question seemed to set the theme for the entire evening. It didn't take me long to come to the realization that I was far better equipped to address the aim of man as it relates to the cleaning of the toilet bowl than I was to talk about man as the ultimate and final aim of the universe.

Eventually we managed to turn the topic of conversation to the subject of friendship which was, in fact, the very reason for inviting Ernie Jr. and Barb to dinner in the first place. Apparently, they too had tried to establish relationships with other couples and had struck out.

"Tom and Beth?" Barb said. "Nothing in common. *They* majored in music!"

Ernie's turn. "Alex and Jane?" Again nothing in common. "They have a baby. We can't even *think* baby at this point."

"Earl and Jessie? Into sports!" *Worse than being into the occult!* was implied by the tone in Barb's voice.

"We thought we had something going with Paul and Ann," Barb continued wistfully. "They're in school too, both in doctoral programs, but you know what the problem is? We're majoring in different things. Totally different interests!"

At last, we said our good-byes with no empty "let's-do-it-again" promises. Wayne and I headed for the kitchen.

"Wonder what they'll say about us? 'That poor Buchanan woman didn't even know what anthropology is!'"

"As you can see, I'm up to my elbows here in the reality of human behavior as it applies to the physical, social, and cultural development of man," Wayne said in mock seriousness, as he scoured a saucepan in the much too greasy dishwater.

"Right," I responded, sopping wet dishrag in hand. "This is a hands-on, scientific interpretation of reality in light of human values and experience."

We bantered on. "Let me ask you a question, a question that could determine how we interpret the reality of the universe as a marital unit." By now the last dish was put away and I was exaggerating my words and teasing my husband, through the living room, down the hall. "Exactly, what *is* your preference when it comes to the ironing and starching of sheets and pillowcases? Because when all is said and done, I'm not at all sure that you and I—the two of us—have anything in common whatsoever."

With that I took a flying leap into the middle of the bed and he was right behind me.

"I think we do!" he answered. "I think we do!"

Chartotte

Friends don't always present themselves as pretty, polite, punctual, and politically correct! One of the most poignant of friendship stories is *Charlotte's Web*, the children's story in which Wilbur the pig observes Charlotte's repugnant, spider qualities —"fierce, brutal, scheming, bloodthirsty." And she eats flies! Yuk!

But buried beneath that rather grisly exterior is a keen intelligence and an underlying spirit of generosity, compassion, and kindness, which ultimately save her friend's life. No wonder millions of us have fallen in love with her!

In the finest of relationships, the object of our adoration is capable of being pushy, impatient, persnickety, and downright pigheaded. Oh, to possess a Wilbur-like wisdom that will allow me to see beyond my friends' faults!

Man looketh on the outward appearance, but the Lord looketh on the heart. 1 Samuel 16:7 KJV

It's good to have friends. I'd hate to think that when I die, they'd have to hire pallbearers.

Metamorphosis

The spring is metamorphosing into
summer,
And I can feel the dry and leathery skin
That encased me through the winter
Getting much too tight and troublesome
For comfort.
I want out!
Out into the fragrant breeze
That soon will dry the natal
moisture
From my wings,
Out into the sun
From which I'll draw
The energy to fly.

And fly I will!
And as I soar,
I'll saturate my mind
With sounds of love and peace,
Everything that moves or breathes.
I'll smell the fragrance of the earth
And kiss the wind
And taste the brand of honey
Every blossom has to offer;
Yet I'll be sure to hear
The silence that the warm and welcome
Evening brings,
And in it I will race with shadows
Just to see which one of us
Can tiptoe in more softly
'Cross the grass.
(I'll walk so gently,
Even you won't
Hear me pass.)

And knowing as I do
The days can't last,
That winter will return too soon,
I'll do and hear and think
And taste it all!
I'll store up multicolor memories
To take me through
The long, gray days
Of winter.

Gloria

Planting the Seeds of Friendship

Great gardens require seeds, and a successful gardener has to know a seed when she sees one. She must learn that seeds are as different and varied as the plants they will ultimately produce.

We learn to recognize the seeds of friendship from those modeled by our parents and other adults, from our childhood experiences (like our first best friends), and from those first broadening experiments with Girl Scouts, 4-H, youth camp, and junior high school.

We learn that some seeds are carried on the wind and seem to blow into our lives as delightful surprises. Good gardeners love seeds as good friends learn to love people. Both have come to know that great plants and great friendships arise from an almost infinite variety of backgrounds and environments, and that given a fighting chance, come spring, they explode into a wonder of life and beauty.

Seeds are the symbolic heart of friendship—unassuming, even drab, indistinct contents of paper packets. Little hopes that are waiting to be nurtured to full bloom.

Together Through Thick and Thin

My friend Joy is the most organized person I know. Her refrigerator is organized, her desk is organized, her silverware is organized, her linen closet is organized, and even her underwear drawer is organized. Can you imagine? As far as I can tell, the only thing she hasn't been able to organize is her husband.

Peggy is our storyteller and our historian. She remembers everything, and if she doesn't remember, she makes it up or exaggerates to make a good story even better. "Remember when you took my jacket to the resale shop by mistake . . . and I had to go get it back . . . and the lady said it was the ugliest jacket she ever saw?" And, "Remember when we put the wrong kind of soap in the dishwasher and we were up to our knees in bubbles?" If the truth were known, we were probably only up to our *ankles*—but who cares? It's Peggy's story! In the unlikely event that Peggy pauses to catch her breath and you should ask a question, her answer is always the same, "I've *already* told you more than I know."

Gloria is by far the most intellectual of the four of us. When we meet, the first words out of her mouth are, "Have you read . . ." and then she names a book I've never heard of, much less read. Or she'll ask, "What are you reading?" And I have to admit I'm reading, *All I Ever Needed to Know, I Learned from My Cat.* For the third time!

As for me—I may as well tell you rather than let you hear it from one of these so-called friends of mine—I'm shallow. I'm not the deepest of thinkers. They'll tell you that when Bibles came out in various colors, that's when I began my earthly ministry: coordinating Bibles with clothing.

"Show Sue a dress, a suit, or even a necktie and she'll match it with a Bible," they say. "Poor thing! That's about all she's got goin' for her!"

The four of us are as different as spring, summer, winter, and fall, but we are best friends. Peggy is an inspirational speaker. Joy is a school teacher and an educational consultant, and Gloria (as in

Gaither) is a famous person, having written the lyrics to hundreds of songs and spoken to thousands of people. I'm vice president of a company that produces video, interactive multimedia, and corporate meetings. We are all authors now, but when we met, only Joy had written books, and Gloria was just beginning to write music with her husband Bill, so a shared interest in writing wasn't the reason for our friendship.

We were drawn together more than twenty-five years ago because our husbands worked together in the music business. Usually such friends drift apart once the common cause no longer exists, but our bond has only gotten stronger.

Perhaps the first reason we've stuck together is that we don't always stick together. We aren't jealous of each other. We don't have to invite *everyone* to *everything* or worry that someone gets left out. In years past, Joy and Gloria have vacationed together without Peggy and me; Peggy and Joy often lunch *tête-à-tête*, and occasionally Joy, Peggy, and I have a slumber party without Gloria. (I didn't say we don't gossip about the person who isn't in attendance. I just said everyone can't always be there!)

When Joy, Peggy, and I get together, *yes* we say that Gloria's kitchen cabinets are messy or that we once saw an inch of mold in her cheese bin. And *yes*, when Peggy isn't there, we make snide comments about the fact she wears a size two and that her jacket was truly ugly! And of course, when Joy isn't around, we conspire to mess up her underwear drawer and say—right out loud—that she'll never get Bob organized and may as well stop wasting her energy!

Catty women that *they* are, I'm sure when I'm not around, *they* bring up the fact that within fifteen minutes of the announcement of the church choir's "tacky party," I got six phone calls from people wanting to borrow my clothes. I say, so what if occasionally—just occasionally, mind you—I buy some glitzy, gaudy jacket, or a pair of big-as-beach-ball earrings. Is this a crime?

The second reason for our long-standing relationship surely must be that we can poke fun at ourselves and at each other. We couldn't do this if there weren't a mutual trust—trust that our motives are pure and whatever we do or say is for fun and not mean-spirited.

Another thing that binds us is a common set of Christian principles—and a lifestyle born of shared values. These are things that drew us together many years ago, and they have never changed. Nor have our priorities—our relationship with God and our commitment to marriage and family. While each of us has a career that challenges and energizes us, we are not defined or consumed by our jobs.

A kind of zany, unexplained, intellectual curiosity is another characteristic we share; yet, as I say the words "intellectual curiosity," I can almost hear my friends shout in unison, "Sue? Curious, yes! Intellectual . . . ?" The question marks hang in the air over their impish faces. The truth is we are all intrigued by "the road less taken." We simply don't want to miss a thing, and to that end, we stretch each other in the pursuit. Sometimes I *do* read those books Gloria recommends!

Friendship such as ours is a rare gift, but it's not without cost. It can be very expensive! Each of us has spent a fortune in greeting cards. Hallmark must love us! My drawers are bulging with cards I've received that are simply too good to throw away. Cards such as "Happy birthday to someone I would never call a dumb blond"— open card—"I know it's not your real color!" Or, "If I had a dollar for every time I thought of you . . . I'd be too filthy rich to have anything to do with you!" And my all-time favorite from Peggy: "You've been with me through all the bad times, all the down times, the worst of times and I just want you to know . . . YOU ARE BAD LUCK!"

Whether or not you call it bad luck, it's true we've been through thick and thin together and I don't mean waistlines. That too! I'm talking about the bad stuff. The death of a husband (Peggy's), the discovery of cancer (mine), the heart attack and surgery of a husband (Joy's), the deaths of all our mothers, and perhaps the most trying of all, children problems! I'll never forget the time we all had cleared our schedules to have an entire, undisturbed day together. We planned to have a big leisurely breakfast at my house, catch up on each other's lives, do a little shopping, eat a late lunch at some nice, cozy tearoom, and maybe catch a movie in the evening. Where we actually ended up was in a heap on the floor, at the top of my stairs. Praying! Because of a major crisis with one of our children—and a couple of potential crises with others—we never made it to lunch or shopping.

The fact that the four of us are bosom buddies doesn't mean we have *an exclusive* on each other. We enjoy multiple friendships outside our circle of four that include church, neighborhood, and business friends. Gloria has close friends in the music community. Joy has close relationships with other educators, and Peggy has more church friends than she can count. I have wonderful friends in the Nashville business community—people who are far more to me than networking opportunities. Each of us has other best friends. I have three best girlfriends from high school—friendships older than dirt!

The key to friendship between women—and somehow for us girls, it's not the easiest thing to achieve—is being able to accept each other unconditionally. If we can do that, the rewards are never ending! And the pay dirt is definitely a bonanza! It's a proven fact we will stay young longer, are less likely to be depressed, and will save a fortune in counseling fees!

If I had to narrow the secret of our friendship to one thought, it would be that *we bless each other,* and within the blessing is a kaleidoscope of meaning—to make happy, to praise, to thank, to protect, to sanctify, to favor, to celebrate, to give benediction. It not only applies to best friends, but it applies to every cherished human relationship—husband and wife, parent and child, sister and brother, neighbor with neighbor, church member with church member. It's cross-cultural, cross-racial, cross-generational, and cross-backyard-fence-*ational*—a made-up word, but that too is allowed with best friends!

Letter to My Cousin

Dear Phoebe:

It was so good to hear from you again. I think so often of the times we sat in the mud puddle at Grandma's house and made the mud pies. Remember the time we mixed dirt with the water from that nice spigot on the barrel and chopped too-ripe cucumbers into our pies—then found out the reason they smelled so strange was because the "water" was kerosene? Remember the times we went berry picking in the woods and picked Grandma's big apron full of the berries that grew out by the old abandoned car where the family of skunks lived?

Remember the old coal-burning cookstove and the warm smell of homemade bread and the taste of fresh-churned butter melted on it? Remember playing Flinch and Dominoes? The smell of kerosene lamps, the taste of potato soup, and the sound of *Clyde Beaty's Circus, The Green Hornet, One Man's Family,* and *Judy Canova* coming from the console radio?

I will never forget Grandma taking down the guitar (Remember how she played it, not like a guitar but like a harp?) and singing songs like

> Blessed assurance Jesus is mine,
> Oh, what a foretaste of glory divine. . . .

When it was time for two little girls to go to sleep she'd put us in that tall, tall bed in that cold, cold room, then cover us with feather-filled comforters that seemed to get everything warm but our noses. And when she thought we were asleep, I can never forget the sound of her kneeling on the linoleum by the rocking chair and the sound of her soft voice praying for us—that somehow God would guide our little lives and protect our souls from the traps of evil. Phoebe, we are indeed rich! Such a heritage. They are fortunate who have ever met a saint. We have walked with one—sat at her knee, touched her silver hair, and felt the warmth of her abundant love. Oh, we weren't so special; she loved every child, every living thing. Her pink carnations and purple morning glories also felt her touch of tenderness. But we are rich because, as the highest of God's creation, He gave us the ability to love back, to return the affection. It is almost as great to be able to love back as it is to know you are loved.

Phoebe, I know you have gone through the doubts and confusion of life so common to those who are struggling to know themselves, just as I have. But the longer I live the more convinced I become that real wisdom and real intelligence and true greatness belong to us only when we get big enough to become as a little child and believe in a Jesus who can make a difference in the way we live. When I compare the life of a saint like Grandma at the end of life to that of a person who has "hoed his own row" all his life, it is about all the proof I need. I don't believe in having a religion, but this thing of serving Jesus, betting everything you are and have on a way that is beyond proof, really works.

Thank God for grandmothers like ours who say to those of us who would doubt—in lives more eloquent than words— "God is real!" Thank you for being a part of the precious memories of my childhood.

Even across the miles and the years I feel very close to you, for the bond of our shared childhood that still holds, ties us at the heart.

With Love,
Gloria

A Belonging Place

There are a lot of good reasons for a person to find a church home. There are the obvious ones: the connection to a place where God is at the center of all that transpires; a place where people who love God can gather and collectively lift their voices in praise and thanksgiving; a place where common people can find an open altar on which to lay their burdens and confess their sins; a place in which to gather themselves and seek to know more of the grace and the power of God in their lives. Does this sound like a list a committee might make up for a brochure?

There is, however, another very good reason for finding a *belonging place* among a group of believers. I found in my belonging place, a place to be needed, to be wanted, to be loved. A place to be connected to others and to God. Finding a place brings purpose and meaning to life. As I think of this connection, I think of the theme song of the television show, *Cheers*. Cheers was a bar—a welcoming place where people knew your name, and everyone was treated the same. The church should be such a place.

At a very young age, through tragedy, I discovered with joy that God's church was my belonging place. One Sunday, when I was twelve years old and my little sister, Joan, was four, we were walking from the bus stop, down the long hill to our house. A man lost control of his car and we were crushed against a stone wall. My little sister died instantly, and I suffered several broken bones, spent months encumbered by casts and crutches, and missed almost an entire year of school. The grief and despair my parents felt was overwhelming. Life for them was never again the same. One of the hardest places for them to go was church. It brought the entire horrifying experience back into their minds. The thought of returning to church where their peer group was busily involved with the normal routine of raising a family was more than they could bear.

It would have been easy for me, a frightened, insecure, over-weight young girl, to slip away, as my parents did, from the protective love of my church.

Thankfully, the Lord was watching over me. This group of believers, many of whom were close personal friends of my parents, literally became my family. They did whatever was necessary to make sure I had every opportunity to participate in the life of the church, whether it was a service or camp meeting, a pageant or Bible quiz, a ball game, or a picnic. I never missed anything!

In those early months, not only did those who included me have an extra kid, they had the baggage of a leg cast, crutches, and a wheelchair. Yet today, my life is so much richer because of their willingness to befriend me. Without realizing it, as I observed their actions and responses, I began to pattern my life after these dear people. Two of them stand out in my mind.

Margaret Griggs was a close personal friend and confidante of my mother. Her daughter, Carolyn, was my age, and together we belonged to a "gaggle of giggling girls" who found fun everywhere we looked—like the many Sunday mornings Aunt Mary Smith would stand up and head to the bathroom in the middle of the sermon. Apparently it wasn't an urgent call, because on her way from the front of the church to the back door, she would stop, at each row to speak to people and inquire about their salvation. I still giggle when I think of it.

The Griggs family, too, enfolded me in their arms and made me belong. Nearly every Sunday until the day she died, Margaret would whisper to me, "You are one of mine and I love you. I believe in you, and you are in my thoughts and prayers. Don't forget us, and come to see us when you can." Margaret Griggs made the church a "Cheers" kind of place for me. She loved me the same way she loved her own family—the way the heavenly Father loves His children. I can still see her face; to me it is the face of Jesus.

Then there was Myrtle Pate, who, in addition to being my Sunday school teacher, friend, and mentor, was the aunt of the best church-league softball pitcher in town—and he just happened to be my heartthrob. I loved to go to the games, in the hope that Jim might look my way, and even cast a smile in my direction. Myrt made sure

I had a ride to the ballpark. I can still see her pulling up in front of my house in her 1940-something Chevy.

Myrt made everything more fun. Her enthusiasm was contagious. Whether she was loading a bunch of silly girls into her car to head for the ball game, practicing a church play that she had written, or teaching us the Scriptures, she gave her all.

As I have matured, her presence in my life has remained important wherever life has taken us. From the soft gentle summer nights at a baseball diamond in Shelby Park to the graveside of both of our husbands, I have drawn courage and strength from this gentle yet strong woman. Her life confirms what she taught me as a young girl, so many years ago—we can put our trust in a sovereign God. We can count on His presence as we learn life's lessons—and press on.

Note to Peg from Gloria: "Our time together this weekend was an amazing thing. It's bigger than we will ever know—an example of a dream that began and ended in the heart of God ... and those dreams have no beginning and no end. My, how I treasure you in my life, my friend."

Knowing a Sprout When You See One

The gardener doesn't see or know the moment the seed begins to throb with the quickening of life, and we often can't pinpoint the moment the seed of friendship first germinates and begins to send out its first fragile roots.

What we can see is the first tender shoot that begins to push its way to the surface. A friendship may sprout during a conversation that strikes a harmonic chord, an unspeakable feeling that two "kindred spirits" have united, or a laugh that reveals a shared sense of humor. Whatever form these first sprouts of relationship take, this is the tentative, experimental season of friendship.

Care must be taken not to bruise the tender shoot by a crushing step or a too-quick weeding. At this stage, the new relationship needs the cultivation of a sensitive ear, the water and feeding of a phone call, or an unexpected thank-you note. A little research may be required to find out what nourishes this new plant or whether it needs protection from predators or the chill of nightfall.

But both friendships and new seedlings are usually tougher than we think and miraculously seem to survive the ignorance and error of the naive gardener. Gardens and friendship both thrive on warmth and light.

That Your Joy Might Be Full

Loving and being loved—being connected, valued, befriended, cherished by another—is a compelling need that permeates the life of every human being on God's earth. Yet neither love nor friendship can be manipulated or prescribed. You can't choose an attractive candidate and merely follow your top-ten list of things to do to make love happen. So how then are such relationships to come about? Is there anything we can do to develop a bond of companionship that is intimate, fulfilling—even joyful?

Jesus Christ created a model of love, as He did of friendship: along with the reassuring "I have loved you even as the Father has loved me . . . I have told you this so that your joy may be full," we hear from His heart the welcoming words, "I have called you friend." Mind-boggling!

I teach creative writing. The first several weeks, my young students spend most of their time learning to use words that *show* rather than *tell*. Creating a visual image of an object or idea precipitates a much stronger response than just telling about it. Brilliant as I may seem (ha!), this is not a concept I just happened to dream up—it's been around a couple of thousand years. The model, again, is Jesus.

When Jesus talked to His disciples, He didn't give long discourses on friendship. He *demonstrated* friendship by being available, compassionate, self-sacrificing, and tender. His chosen friends responded! Yes, He called them to accountability; He rebuked them when they were wrong. But when He was finished, they still felt cherished by Him. What a picture!—another of His gifts to us—to be treasured, to be emulated.

We need not set out in search for a friend . . . rather, we must simply set out to be the friend Christ modeled—anticipating the needs of others, wearing ourselves out at giving. *Jesus died doing it.* The rewards are infinite and joyous!

Love one another the way I loved you. This is the very best way to love. Put your life on the line for your friends. You are my friends when you do the things I command you. . . . Remember the root command: Love one another. John 15 THE MESSAGE

And So I Was

Do you remember when you were a kid, lying on your back in the grass, discovering pictures in the clouds? Remember how you and your "best friend ever" would often see the same object? That's the way you *knew* she was your best friend ever. You saw things alike! That quality is one of the first memories I have of Joy MacKenzie. We saw things the same way. We still do. Perhaps it's because we both have a rather warped sense of humor!

Our idea of a great day is making a plan to do something fun together. An even greater day is being so busy sitting on the couch or lying on the bed (or better yet, lying on a beach) talking that, because we become so engrossed in our conversation, we wind up scrapping our original plan—and just keep talking. And talking! And talking!

This girl (she will always be a girl to me) brightens my life! She sees the world through the eyes of a child, and I hope she never grows up. The simple pleasure of being together is all that we need to have a good time. Often we spend our days laughing and being silly; sometimes we cry. The important thing is that there are no instructions, no "ought-tos" or "shouldn'ts." No lessons, no rules. We just *are*. My times with Joy have been some of the mountaintop experiences of my life. They are moments that cause my heart to rejoice.

I'll never forget the first time we met. It was at the World's Fair in New York City. We found each other fun and interesting from day one, but on that day, we also thought we would never see each other again. Little did we suspect our husbands would wind up in business together and our lives would be intertwined for over thirty years. That hot summer day, which we assumed would be our first and last together, we told each other everything we knew. In fact we told each other *more* than we knew!

You can imagine how surprised I was when my husband called me months later to say the MacKenzies were moving to Nashville. Everything I had said to her that day at the fair flooded into my memory. Like a drowning man, I felt I was going under for the third time. Immediately, I got on the phone to let her know how happy we would be to have them in Nashville but also to say, "I just want you to know that, in New York, I gave you the *Reader's Digest* version of my stories. When you get here, I'll fill in any details you wish. But if you *ever* breathe one word to anyone, I'll have to kill you!"

From that day to this, we've told each other many secrets, and never once have I been concerned about her keeping my confidence. She is totally trustworthy—a genuine friend. She is also a veritable source of knowledge and information—often more than you asked for or wanted—but one of those great people who loves fun, food, fellowship, chocolate, and beach bumming! And did I mention talking? (After all, aren't those the virtues most important in a friend?) Through the years, Joy has prayed for me, energized me, believed in me, nudged me. If you want to know the truth, she has *shoved* me! She saw something in me years ago that I didn't have confidence to see for myself. When I think of her influence in my life, I remember the quote from a little boy who wrote of his teacher, "My teacher thought I was better than I was, and *so I was.*"

My Kind of Woman

She was our first child's kinder-garten teacher. We met her when we took Suzanne to visit school for Kinder-garten Roundup. She was a buxom, cheerful woman with a happy smile and that special precise and enunciated way of speaking that almost always identifies those who teach ele-mentary children. Her name was Ione Craig.

Even though Suzanne was usually slow to warm up to strangers, she took to Mrs. Craig right away. We felt relieved that our first child was going to have a smooth adjustment to this new environment. At the time, Bill was serving on our local school board, so it made him happy to feel that the school had such great teachers on staff.

The first few weeks of school Bill and I took turns picking up Suzanne. Bill tried to pick her up most often, since I had two babies at home—a one-year-old and another not quite three months. It seemed, however, as though every time Bill would try to leave the office to pick up Suzanne, there'd be an important phone call or a meeting would hold him over, and he'd arrive at the Marie Thurston Elementary School five or ten minutes late.

One day toward the end of the second week of school, Bill was again late. Soon Suzanne came to the car alone with a note pinned to her sweater. Bill unpinned the piece of paper and read this message:

Dear Mr. Gaither:

School is dismissed at 11:20. It is very upsetting for the children when no one is here to pick them up when the other children are picked up. From now on I shall expect you to be here promptly at 11:20.

Sincerely,
Ione Craig

Bill brought the note home and read it to me with great delight. "I love that!" he said. "This teacher doesn't care about my being on the school board or anything else I do. She is only concerned about the well-being of her kids. That's my kind of woman. I want us to get to know her!"

We did get to know her. There was the day Suzanne came home so excited she couldn't stop talking about the finger painting project she'd done that day. "And, Mother, we didn't have to use just our fingers! We could use our elbows or arms or toes or knees. . . ." she bubbled. "And when we were done, Mrs. Craig said we could lick the paint off if we wanted to."

"Lick it?" I asked.

"Yes!" sang Suzanne. "The paint was chocolate pudding!"

This teacher found all kinds of ways to make a child's first experiences with learning great fun. When the snow came that winter, I went early one day to pick up Suzanne. As I waited, parked by the curb, I noticed an adult body and fifteen little bodies, clad in snowsuits and ski suits lying on their backs in the front school yard in the deep snow. Legs and arms moved in and out, up and down.

"Snow angels!" Suzanne squealed when she got to the car. "We made angels in the snow! Mrs. Craig made the biggest angel!"

It wasn't long before Ione became part of a Bible study group that met at my mother's house. I found her insights into Scripture to be as refreshing as her teaching methods. The Word of God was alive and breathing in the "daily" of her life, and she was full of examples of how God speaks through His Word.

One morning she called my house. There were tears in her tone, a deep sadness. "Have you checked your martin boxes this morning?" she asked. Ione and I shared a love for birds and I'd found her to be quite an authority on their songs and habits. "No, I haven't been out yet," I answered. "What's wrong?"

"The city fogged for mosquitoes last night," she said. "The mother martins fed the poisoned mosquitoes to their babies, and this morning all the baby birds are dead in their nests." The compassion and grief in her voice reminded me of Jesus' words: "Not one sparrow falls without my Father's notice," and I knew both God and Ione would grieve today for what we had done to our environment. How ironic that we had killed the very birds that eat thousands of mosquitoes a day.

Much later when my mother was recovering from knee-replacement surgery, Ione offered to share her room at the Praise Gathering for Believers, the annual event that Bill and I are responsible for each year in Indianapolis, and see that Mother got to all the events. "You two have too much to do that weekend," she told us. "I'd love to have Dorothy go with me; then we can talk about everything."

By then not only had Ione been Suzanne's friend for over twenty years, but she had become a treasured friend of our whole family and had endeared herself to a wide circle of our friends. Bill asked her if she would like to lead the early morning prayer time at Praise Gathering. She agreed and helped several hundred people begin their day, focused on the God who walks and laughs and cries with us. And makes angels! And chocolate! And baby martins!

One morning she told this story. She had given her children the assignment of writing love notes for Valentine's Day. "Kindergartners can't write much yet, but they all can write 'I love you,'" she said. One little guy had written this note to Ione: "You are the bust, bust, bust teacher in the world. I love you."

Ione's husband, Armond, read the letter, then chuckled to himself. "There's nothing wrong with his spelling," he told her. "The kid just can't count!"

I'm not quite sure how Ione managed to weave that story into her morning devotions. I *do* know that she believed that God had a great sense of humor and that He loved us enough to give us a great deal to laugh about.

Ione is now retired from teaching, but she goes on teaching just the same. The last letter I received from her she told how exciting her volunteer work is. She's teaching reading and literacy to adults who somehow fell through the cracks in our educational system.

And she is traveling all over the world—places like Australia, New Zealand, Scandinavia, and the Baltic. On her most recent trip she was stuck in an airport for more than twenty-four hours. Most of the travelers were pretty bent out of shape about this, that is, until Ione and her sister made a table out of their carry-on bags, pulled out a checkerboard and a deck of cards and started challenging fellow travelers to a checker and Rook tournament.

Although my friendship with Ione sprouted unexpectedly in the surprising soil of a kindergarten classroom, she has come to be a beautiful and enduring flower in my garden of friends. She has taught me the wonderful lesson to bloom wherever there is a patch of soil, and spread to seeds of friendship wherever the winds of opportunity blow. If I had to draw a picture of Ione's spirit, it would look like a milkweed seed with wings attached . . . a whole lot like an angel.

Any one of us can do a little digging, be diligent enough with the watering can, keep an eye out for weeds, and with the help of the Gardener, we can begin to have a little something bloom in our lives—something like patience or peace or discipline or love or joy—something simple and beautiful, like a new friendship. Something that will help us to take heart on the days when the storms come. Something that may cause a friend to reward us by saying, "My, what pretty flowers!"

from *Listening for a God Who Whispers*

A Letter to Suzanne
—upon her decision
to become a photographer, at age 14!

Dear Suzanne,

I hear you have decided to be a real, honest-to-goodness photographer. I feel it is my responsibility to give you some tips I've picked up along the way.

Don't forget to put film in the camera. I once shot towering church steeples, surrounded by snow-covered pine boughs. For two hours I shot, my fingers nearly dropping off from the cold, only to find I hadn't come to the end of the roll because I'd never put the film in the camera!

Use lots of film and take lots of pictures. Throw the bad ones away and only show the good ones. If you do show the bad ones, be sure to say they are "arty" and that you charge more for "arty" ones.

When you work in the darkroom, it isn't enough to just shut your eyes . . . Turn off the lights!

Be careful with whom you choose to go to the darkroom, and when your mom asks you what you were doing in there, you'd better have some prints to show her.

Remember to shoot pictures of girls and women once in awhile . . . not just cute guys. Last year I shot pictures at a large company in Chicago, and when I got back to Nashville, I had seven rolls of one man. The man is very handsome and quite witty, and Wayne knows him. Since then, I've been assigned to roll film in the lab.

You can get in just about any place free now. Just hang your camera around your neck, look official, and say, "Press." If that doesn't work, *hit them with your camera.*

Let me know if you need any more help! Have a good year!

Love,
Sue

A Place at the Table

Peggy

I'd lost touch with an old family friend, even though she lives near my walking path. Early one morning, she caught me peeping over her fence at her lovely shade garden. After we laughed at my startled embarrassment and reintroduced ourselves, she invited me in to see her English tea service and antique doll collection. It was such fun to see Alice again in her lovely home and to renew an old friendship. As I went through the kitchen toward the back door and the garden gate, I noticed she had her kitchen table set properly for two ... I apologized for taking her time when it was obvious she was expecting company. "I'm not expecting company," she said. "I set the table right after breakfast, just in case my husband comes home for lunch. It's such a special treat for me when he can get away from the office, I want to be prepared, *just in case*. Ready at a moment's notice!"

This incident reminded me of my good friend, Maylou, who lives in Europe. Maylou comes from a minister's family where proper manners and table graces were taught to young children and practiced as long as the child remained in the house. Therefore, she knows from her parents' example how to treat a guest.

If I had to describe Maylou in a few short sentences, it would be tough to do. She has so many interesting facets to her personality. I have had the privilege of being in her home several times over the years. Being in her home is like going to a four-star hotel, or in Europe, a Romantique hotel, only warmer and more personal. The moment you walk in you realize she is thinking only of you and is offering the gift of her home and herself. You are not an intrusion or an afterthought. She has prepared the table—fine china and linen; the bedroom—books and fresh flowers; the bathroom—soft towels and sweet-smelling soap. All is made ready, with you and your comfort in mind.

Then there is the fun part of Maylou! One reason we get along so well is because we are both talkers (as opposed to listeners)! We can both hold our own when it comes to making conversation. We share the same motto: *No talk is too small for me!*

We don't have the opportunity to see each other very often, and when we do, we cherish every minute. We sit cross-legged in the middle of the bed and talk and talk. We share stories and pictures of children and grandchildren. We laugh and tell tales of crazy stuff we used to do together when we were young and foolish. We share our dreams and hopes for ourselves and our families. It's as if for a moment, time stops and we have never been parted. We spread our lives out like a road map and trace where we've been, where we are, and where we would like to be, and for the time that we have together, hostess Maylou and guest Peggy are family.

Like my found-again friend Alice, Maylou is prepared. She sets about to make sure her friends know they are welcome. Not only is there a place for you at her table, but there is a place for you in her heart as well. She welcomes you with open arms, a big smile, and a strong hug. Now that's a perfect hostess and a lovely, gracious friend. Ready at a moment's notice!

> *I've loved you the way my Father has loved me. Make yourself at home in my love. . . . This is my command. Love one another the way I have loved you.* John 15 THE MESSAGE

In a Garden
You Can Hear God Laughing

Like people, plants are born with personality. The difference, I think, is that in His plan for people, God added humor!

Some plants feed upon a seed beneath the earth. Others push the seed case forth—some with methodical care, others with reckless abandonment.

I am often gently nourished by a friend whose quiet company provides wisdom and comfort for my spirit.

I am sometimes coquettishly coaxed from my comfortable environment and persistently urged through the crusty surface soil by sister, Marge, or Lynn (my "crocus"), or Gloria.

But on occasion, I have been catapulted from my warm bed to worlds beyond my experience by the likes of my professional colleague, Kathy, often by my mother or my husband, Bob.

We nurture and are nourished by our friends in different ways. In His plan for friends, I think God often paints way outside the lines. The color may not rival that of the flower garden, but the comedy is superb!

Research tells us that if you're a talker, you'll choose a willing listener as a best friend. Boy, are they wrong! Sue's husband has offered, on many occasions, to go along on our "women only" soirees—just so there would be someone to listen.

Maintenance Tips for a Friendship Garden

Forgive easily. Some people seem to draw imaginary lines in the imaginary sand and then wait for the other person to *mess up*—to cross that line. Another friend or potential friend is then x-ed from the list. "I saw it coming. I was just waiting for it to happen. I can't seem to make (or keep) friends. One more person let me down, didn't measure up to my standards!" *My standards?* Excuse me! Who am I to set standards? Perhaps a better way of thinking would be to forgive the other person—isn't there something in the Bible about that?—before she's even aware that your imaginary line exists! Get the chip off your shoulder. Forgive easily. After all, you don't want imaginary friends, do you?

Don't rule anyone out as a potential friend. Sometimes we think a friend has to be "just like me!" She should be from *my neighborhood*. After all, I don't want to go too far out of my way. She should be in *my income bracket*. What if she has better stuff than I do? How about this one: She should be from *my church*? I'd hate to spend the rest of my life setting her straight, correcting her theology, and worrying whether she'll be in heaven because she's been dunked or splashed! The four of us—Peggy, Gloria, Joy, and Sue—don't go to the same brand of church and don't agree on every theological nuance. For instance, eternal security. You should hear us debating that one!

Want to be a friend? Think twice! It's one of those days—already full of frustrations. The telephone rings. Someone you care about has a need. Can you possibly fit just one small favor into your already-too-full schedule?

Strong friendships almost always involve self-sacrifice. People who don't wish to be inconvenienced or embarrassed or deal with a long, long list of other impositions and annoyances don't usually endure. Almost every human relationship is messy once in awhile. Being a real friend means giving freely and expecting nothing in return. That's the Christ model!

Have friends or die! Someone has said that America is in the midst of a loneliness epidemic and that it's undermining our health. But wait! Aren't we supposed to be strong and self-reliant? Isn't loneliness a sign of weakness? Recent studies by major universities indicate that health problems we call "depression" and "low self-esteem" could just as accurately be called "loneliness." These same studies say that people who have friends live longer, have fewer illnesses, and that a close circle of friends actually helps the immune system work. With this in mind, run, don't walk, to your nearest neighborhood coffee klatch, church group, political club, or neighborhood bar. (Just kidding about the bar, but you get the drift!) You won't find that "close circle of friends," sitting at home reading *National Enquirer* and watching TV! You do want your immune system to work, don't you?

Summer's Splendor

... Friendship
in Bloom

The Budding of Friendship

If the soil is right and the weather holds, the gardener has little to do with the amazing miracle of growth. Below the surface, roots are deepening, spreading, drawing nourishment to make tall, strong stems. The gardener only needs to recognize and appreciate the infinite variety, color, and uniqueness of the new plants and give each the chance to do its own thing.

Invitation to a Feast

Joy

C. S. Lewis says of friendship, "Christ, who said to the disciples, 'Ye have not chosen me, but I have chosen you,' can truly say to every group of Christian friends, 'You have not chosen one another but I have chosen you for one another.' The Friendship is not a reward for our discrimination and good taste in finding one another out. It is the instrument by which God reveals to each the beauties of all the others. They are no greater than the beauties of a thousand other men; by Friendship, God opens our eyes to them. They are, like all beauties, derived from Him and then, in a good Friendship, increased by Him through the Friendship itself so that it is His instrument for creating as well as for revealing. At this feast it is He who has spread the board and it is He who has chosen the guests. It is He, we may dare to hope, who sometimes does and always should, preside. Let us not reckon without our Host."

It is a sumptuous table at which I sit! The feast God has spread before me is far more lavish than I could ask or think.

I have closed my eyes and imagined myself at a banquet table, opulent as one I once saw in a movie. At this feast in my mind were seated a revered host of diners whom I could identify as close, intimate friends, each chosen by a God who anticipated my every need and personally supervised the arrangement of place cards at the table.

Of course there was Peg, of whom I never tire—comfortable for me, like furry bedroom slippers, maybe with funny faces on the front. Sue, God knew I needed for fun and off-the-wall stimulation. Gloria, He chose for my intellectual challenge and soul mate.

Across the table, I saw my sister-in-law, Carol. We became confidantes as co-commiserators in the painful, early years of marriage. Washing dishes after those sumptuous, holiday feasts prepared by our mother-in-law, we always found time to talk about the broader aspects of relationships, explore new ideas, and review books we'd read.

In the early, child-rearing years, my place was between Shirley and Susan in a neighborhood where our homes became a three-part playground for children and where we would grow up together as mothers. We still get together for lunch now and then, just to celebrate having survived those hectic years.

Minnie, my angel, sat in a place of honor. In her, I found a family prayer warrior and co-mother to my children (the one to whom they actually listened!). Next to Minnie was Evelyn, mother of all mothers, my travel buddy and photographer *extraordinaire*—chronicler of all the important events of our lives. And for the moments when I have needed an intimate oneness, there was Marty, whose evenness and maturity always make it feel good to be with her.

That noisy group at the other end of the table was made up of my Fellowship Group brothers and sisters—a vital life-support system for our family. The one with the twinkle in his eye (and a computer manual in his hand) would be Wayne, my fellow PK (and Sue's husband). We are each other's safety valve when Bob and Sue are on a tear.

Then there was Bill (G-G-Gaither) No one keeps better track of his friends. He calls often just to check in, encourage, and tell a joke that makes you laugh *ahead* of the stuttered punch line. Long-distance friends Fred and Lois are good at touching base too—calling to say, "We're here; we care!" Their generosity in loaning us their vacation home has often provided a hiding place for soothing the weariness of life's frenzied moments—and for writing books.

Hovering just above the table, close to my chair, was Bob Benson. I wasn't surprised at the location; with our shared meat-and-potatoes appetites, we always engineered near proximity at such functions so we could work out a strategy for ejecting yukky food. With his new access to extraterrestrial information, I hope he's still the president of my fan club. (Hey, in his present state, perhaps he could carry off those cabbage soufflés and brussel sprout canapés unnoticed!)

Looking about this feast table, I was giddy with delight that God chose to place closest to me my sister, Marge—my rock, my friend most constant, selfless and trustworthy, the one on earth who loves me most unconditionally. And I blushed to think of barren days when I had felt intense loneliness. How could one feel friendless in the midst of such company? Amidst such joy, why have I so often chosen self-pity? I am haunted by images of myself as overworked, unappreciated, misunderstood, emotionally abandoned. Over and over again, like old tapes, my mind replays phrases like "I work my fingers to the bone; rarely does anyone say, 'Thank you.'" "Nobody cares how *I* feel." "No one asks what *I* need." "Is there such a thing as a shelter for abused mothers?" "My husband doesn't listen to me." "If school administrators had to spend just *one* day as a classroom teacher . . ." Whoa! In the center of all this chaos (much of which is real and justifiably frustrating) there *is*, " . . . derived from a gracious heavenly Father and increased by Him, . . ." *a feast table!*

It is easy to be impressed by the tangible blessings that grow from such friendships; the merriment, the muscle, the food, the phone calls, the comfortableness are reinforcing. But the accelerated pace and pressure of daily life, with its disappointments, make it tougher to faithfully associate such personal fulfillment with the goodness of a God whose ever-presence pours such blessing on us— just because He loves us!

Lord, make me increasingly aware that to be chosen by You also includes Your choices of those who nurture me in ways too many and magnificent for me to imagine. The feast at which I am sitting is more luxurious than I can comprehend. My simple table blessing is inadequate, but . . . thank you!

Friend in a Café

I was in a small café in Sweden having coffee one morning. The waitress was not Swedish, but Spanish, and spoke both Swedish and English. As she wiped off the table with a sponge, then stopped to take my order, there was no barrier between us. She was a woman, doing what I had done a thousand times. She made coffee in the mornings, got her children off to school, and tried to make ends meet at the market. She was very bright; her snapping eyes told me that. Yet she served. She managed things there in the café. She was capable of more.

Gloria

What we exchanged across a cultural barrier was instant friendship because we shared a kinship with women everywhere. Women have always been able to make do out of what life hands them, to create an ordered universe in the midst of chaos and stress. Women have always been able to make something from nothing, stretching the stew, making the worn-out clothes or opportunities into something *new*, smiling and caressing in spite of their own inclinations to give in to tears and fatigue, mothering the world. Yet, like the new friend I made in the café, while their hands were performing the task at hand, their minds were racing on. Assimilating. Analyzing. Philosophizing.

Someone has said that men are effective while women are reflective. That may be true. So much of men's thinking is applied directly to their work. The result of their thinking is output, income, product. But much of what women think about does not create tangible product. Historically, their assigned roles in society have prevented this. Instead, they ponder the meaning and quality of life. Such pondering may not result in consumable products, but it can produce great souls—souls who ask *why* instead of merely *what* and *how*. Women, after all, are about the industry of the heart.

True friends stretch each other. The four of us are good at that and have the stretch marks to prove it!

The Full Bloom of Friendship

*To friendships in full bloom, we are water bearers, thirst
quenchers, draught doctors, warriors against pestilence, cus-
todians, pullers of weeds, and pruners of spent blossoms—
also gatherers of harvest!*

Finding Time for Friendship

It has occurred to me that, in a given day or week, I bear the titles, the rewards, and the responsibilities of multiple people.

In the short space of one afternoon, I have often been called on to fulfill an amazing assortment of roles that include—for starters—the roles of wife, mother, daughter, sister, teacher, writer, housekeeper, cook, recreation director, receptionist, and referee. By evening, I am ready to be "roled" away!

I am all those people! I am capable of playing each of those roles effectively—with enthusiasm—but not on the same day!

On a given day, I am a fine mother and a devoted wife. At the same time, I can operate a respectably clean and organized household, answer the phone, and be responsible for planning and executing the activities of a busy family. On rare occasions, I may even satisfy those roles and teach a full school day; in an exceptional moment, I might throw in one of my famous box cakes or five-minute Campbell's-based casseroles as a bonus! But on that day, I am going to have no uninterrupted time to spend on the phone with my sister, to counsel or enjoy a leisurely lunch with a friend, or to get any serious writing done.

Unfortunately, none of the above jobs are either optional or part-time. Most require full-fledged concentration and energy. So how does one fit *friend* into this already staggering roster of responsibility? Often, when I look at my calendar, it amazes me that, in the grand scheme of things, I have any friends at all. Of course, there is only one reasonable explanation for the great gift of true friendship, and that lies in the Maker of the Universe who has drawn every minute plan for my life. However, if I wish to be a gracious recipient of His gift—nourish, protect, and enjoy it as delights the Giver—then I do have some responsibility in the matter!

There is no clear-cut, how-to, success-guaranteed program for true friendship, but I recognize in the extraordinary relationships of my life some consistencies that have made friendship enduring.

First, I have only a few close friends. We're not talking casual acquaintances here. We're talking people who know me inside out—people I could trade panty hose with, people I can trust with my darkest secret, my most delicate china, and my wildest dream. People for whom I don't have to put on makeup or straighten the house.

Second, only low-maintenance friends qualify for the short list: I can cut short a telephone conversation without explanation; I can NOT invite them to a dinner party, and they know I must have a good reason; they don't get bent out of shape when I forget to pick up their kids on the way to the game, as I promised, or forget to retrieve *mine* from *them* after the game. They never demand more than I can give and are willing to let me sacrifice for them when they are in need. (I know lots of folks who are exceptionally generous givers but so bloomin' self-sufficient that they would die before they let a friend return a favor. A good friend is also a gracious receiver!)

Lastly, I find that my best friends are those with whom the give-and-take is joyful and genuine—people with whom I can be my whole self, hiding neither warts nor marks of beauty, and with whom selflessness is never a chore. We are as happy for one another's successes as we are sad for failures. (Surprisingly, that's not easy for human beings!)

Through the maze and amazement of many years of relationships, I have learned that all friends aren't meant to be for a lifetime. In the garden of friendship, too, there are annuals and perennials. Some demand careful tending while others flourish with little attention. It helps to remember that though human relationships, like flowers, require human intervention, a sovereign Master Gardener is in charge. He plans not only the original mix of genus, color, height, fullness, and durability, but He knows exactly in what space at what time each can bloom to its full potential and complement and nourish (or draw nourishment from) the others. And when the garden's self-sustaining cycle is diminished, He lovingly makes divine provision for rest and regeneration. Yes, friendship has its seasons, only one of which is spring!

> *To every thing there is a season, and a time to every purpose under the heaven.* Ecclesiastes 3:1 KJV

P.S. At the beginning of this piece, I neglected to mention my role as gardener. At this writing, most of my flowering plants are listless, begging for attention; but my weeds are staunch and healthy. Perhaps next year, I'll trade my high-maintenance flower bed in for a no-maintenance weed garden!

Peg's wish is that once before she dies, she would like to have everything in order: her closets, her pantry, the basement. She would like to have her garden weeded, her checkbook balanced, her "To Do" list done, her will current, her tithe paid, her roots covered, her nails manicured, all the mending finished, the notes she'd meant to write to her friends written ... Oh well, she pretty much lives in a dream world anyway!

Annuals

In the garden of friendship there will be annuals. These are
flowers that bloom most brightly for their season but will not
survive the first frost. Annuals must be watered, fertilized,
and sometimes pinched back to remove spent blossoms and
encourage new growth, but the reward for this special care
is a riot of pizzazz and outrageous color. Save the seeds.
These varieties are worth replanting!

A Riot of Color

Annuals are characterized by their showiness and their brilliant colors. They need very little care. In the course of life I've been pleasantly surprised to find that given the right conditions, climate, and care, an annual can become a perennial. The same can be said for a friend. Sue, my showy annual, has become my perennial friend. What can be said about such an outrageously funny, warm, creative, *dippy* person? At first meeting Sue might appear to be just another pretty face, a flash in the pan, or even a good-time party girl who never has a serious thought or care in the world. In reality she is a solid, deeply rooted perennial whose worth and value is no imitation. She's the real thing! I often remind her that for a shallow person, she is very deep!

Sue is a nonconformist, a free spirit, yet she is compassionate, caring, and accepting of others. You see, she knows and understands about pain and suffering and sorrow. Together, we have lived through some very dark days: the fourteen long years of my husband's cancer and subsequent death and Sue's own struggle with breast cancer and chemotherapy. We have seen one another's best and worst: me with no makeup, dark circles around my dark circles, gray roots showing, flat chest and skinny, ninety-four-pound frame (right after Bob's death), and my trademark buckteeth, which she has always been kind enough not to mention. I have seen her with makeup smeared and smudged in her crow's-feet, dark roots, artificial nails chewed off—though not from gardening—and one breast missing (only briefly, before reconstructive surgery).

When Bob was ill, especially during those last days in the hospital, Sue was dealing with her own mortality. Visiting a dying man was beyond her powers just then, and yet she wanted me to know her heart and prayers were with me. She would send me notes via the nuns at St. Thomas Hospital. One such note said, "At lunchtime today, I stopped in at the chapel to pray for Bob and especially for you. I asked the Lord to give you strength and courage and sustaining grace." She was touched by my grief and wasn't afraid to say so.

Her courage has been an example for me to follow in the grieving process. Sue's warm open ways, her spontaneous comments, and her effervescent presence have endeared her to me. Any excuse to see Sue is enough for me; she is one of those larger-than-life people who takes up lots of room in your heart and life. In a motel room she takes up *all* the bathroom countertop space. We tell her it takes a lot of makeup to look that good!

How much do I love her? I'm the only friend she has who will actually volunteer to share a motel room with her when a group of us is traveling. The sound of her snoring is second only to the take-off of a 747. She is utterly impossible! Impossible, that is, not to love!

Minnie Hill

What I remember most about her were her lemon pies and fried chicken, her grape arbor, heavy with its purple harvest, and the player piano, the pedals of which I could scarcely reach. And her hands—hands that loved the earth like she loved people, hands cracked into little rivers as only years of tender digging in the soil can do. Her flowers and her fruit trees, her grapevines and tomato plants responded to those hands much like the children in her class responded to her love.

Gloria

She wasn't the world's greatest teacher, professionally speaking, but what she lacked in method she abundantly made up for in tender concern. She said so much by living that even a musty basement classroom, chalk dust, and old Sunday school papers were powerless to muffle her message.

"God loves you. He has put you here for a reason, and life's only purpose is to find that reason and fulfill it." We heard. And most were obliged to do something about it.

God's grace and mercy make good friends possible.

Surprised by Friendship

When you're feeling fat, tired, and chronically ordinary, you don't need a friend who is strikingly attractive, perfectly accessorized, and works out every day at five. If I had had any idea that Carlana and I were going to become lifelong friends, I'd have gone to charm school and started aerobic training at age twelve.

She's the kind of person who can rinse and stack the dishes, then run out to the garbage can in the rain in a silk dress and remain spotless—the type women love to idolize in magazines, but dread being seated next to at a formal dinner.

This was not a friendship sought by either of us. It was one of those husband-introduces-wife-to-friend's-wife-then-disappears deals. Bob had just joined the Benson Company as the creative director, and Carlana's husband, Joe, was the piano player and spokesman for a popular southern gospel quartet, The Imperials. The occasion was an all-night Southern Gospel Singin', and the scene was one of those backstage frenzies during which wives were *parked* in the wings for a very long evening.

Carlana, raised a southern Methodist, was familiar with the All-Night Singin' *savoir faire*. Heretofore, I, a conservative, Baptist preacher's daughter, raised in Michigan, thought gospel singing was the music of George Beverly Shea. Carlana, dressed to the nines, knew every person who passed our neat little lineup of off-stage chairs. I, Miss Plain Jane, recognized no one. We were an unlikely pair!

I did my best to smile, rather than stare, as she interacted with a cavalcade of performers who came and went, came and went, came and went. *Surely, I am dreaming,* I thought. *I am a player in a theatrical farce; why else would I feel like a war orphan in the company of royalty?*

Will I never learn that in life's theater, the producer is a sovereign God who creates unthinkable and even preposterous scenarios to accomplish His purposes? Why would I not guess, sitting there in my backstage seat, that He, with a twinkle in His eye, was planning for me and this too perfectly coifed woman, an enduring friendship?

Thirty years later, I have come to understand the value of His gift. In those three decades, we have pushed baby carts through shopping malls, driven coast to coast a number of times with our three children, in pursuit of our workaholic husbands, or occasionally, abandoned them (the husbands, not the children) for a week of building sand castles at the beach. During the years Bob and Joe worked together, we hit our stride—a perfectly matched obsessive-compulsive, highly organized pair, planning and executing dozens of business-related social functions. We supported one another through more than a few tough personal circumstances and watched together, from the safe harbor of our friendship, some turbulent times in the music business.

In recent years, our lives have taken very diverse paths; our time together is limited, and we are no longer an integral part of one another's daily routines. In spite of philosophical distance, we share a trust and mutual devotion born of more than longevity. Mismatched as we started out to be, our friendship has endured, and I find myself pausing often to savor the memory of those early times together.

In a scrapbook of photos commemorating a trip a group of us had taken to Grand Cayman, I recently came across an uncharacteristic candid of a sleeping Carlana. The inscription read: "It's 10:00 A.M. She hasn't washed her face, had devotions, eaten breakfast, or run a mile!" Her traveling companions were delighted to have caught her in such a compromising state!

All these long years after that first backstage meeting, she still looks magazine perfect and works out at five, and I only occasionally feel like the orphan child seated next to the queen.

Perennials

Perennials *take little care. They reseed themselves, grow in a wide variety of environments, and are not delicate or touchy. They bloom profusely and when picked, only bloom the better. They make great bouquets because they don't wilt quickly, and they blend spectacularly with other varieties. Just a little water in any container and they give pleasure to the beholder. Often perennials are considered weeds until recognized by an astute gardener and moved to an environment where their beauty can be displayed to its best advantage. Perennial friendships don't hit their prime in one season; they may take time to bloom and grow, but in the end, they are enduring and dependable.*

My Mother, My Friend

My best, deepest, and longest enduring friendships have been in my own family. From those women closest to me I have learned what friendship is, how to respond to it, and what an important part it can play in the shaping and defining of ourselves.

My first friend was my mother, and from my earliest memories, I knew that she was my friend. This did not mean that she was overpermissive or indulgent. Far from it! She was always tuned in to what I was doing and thinking; she seemed to have eyes in the back of her head. But she was also my ally and made me know that she believed in me and wanted me to win at life.

Gloria

Because she was so energetic and young at heart, my friends considered her one of us. She was their friend and confidante, defender and advocate.

She taught me my first lessons about friendship by being my first, last, and most enduring friend, and although she is gone from this earth, she is far from gone from my life. Her convictions and humor, her openness and adventuresome spirit, her fidelity and endurance, her commitment and resilience have schooled my definition and expectations of friendship.

Now as I remember her, I most remember her hands. I remember her hands almost before I remember her face. I was always aware of hands that could do what needed to be done: smooth, caress, warm, mold, paint, decorate, plant, harvest, demonstrate, sew, press, write, admonish, hug, comfort. Her hands never seemed to be at rest. Even when she slept, it seemed that her hands didn't; they were always on call.

I used to ask her about her hands and she would tell me stories of the scars and dents and mishaps that shaped them, like the time she got her finger caught in the old-fashioned clothes ringer while feeding dish towels into the double rolling cylinders that squeezed the water from the cloth. She recited stories of slicing her thumb with the butcher knife or shutting her finger in the car door. "Beauty marks" are what people used to call the little brown moles on the upper lip of some high school homecoming queen; but I thought the term was better fitted to the "adventure scars" on Mother's hands.

I remember her face. I remember the way it felt when I ran my tiny hands over its flawless smoothness to put myself to sleep. I've observed that most children have something soft and smooth to which they become attached that gives them a sense of security—the smooth satin of a blanket binding, a piece of soft flannel, a small furry stuffed animal. But I touched my mother's face, ran my small hands over her cheeks and neck and lips, and went to sleep knowing she was beside me. Usually she was still reading when I dropped off to sleep, and I knew that she'd doze off for a few minutes, then quietly slip away to finish some job she couldn't do with me awake.

Years later as I cared for her during her last days, I again touched her cheeks, still soft and smooth, and I felt secure. But I did not sleep. She slept. And I knew—we both knew—that although I was awake and watching, it would be she who would soon slip away to complete an assignment only she could do—alone.

I remember her bearing—her dignity, beauty, and self-respect. We used to kid her about being short, though she'd always stretch the truth to make her driver's license read 5'4". Daddy would stand mockingly tall beside her and put his arms around her shoulders as if he had to stretch to reach that far down. She'd pretend to punch him in the stomach and say, "I'm not short; I'm as tall as anybody!" And so she was. My memory of her was that she was straight and "as tall as anybody." She was always well dressed and well groomed. I never remember her wearing a sloppy housecoat or scruffy slippers. When I came downstairs in the morning to the smell of bacon frying in the kitchen I would always find her looking "put together" with her makeup on, hair combed, clothes pressed and coordinated, and wearing her high-heeled shoes. She even worked in the flower garden in high heels, and only when bunion surgery forced her, did she make the concession to wear lower heels; then she refused to wear oxfords or practical flats. Years later, in the hospital, when she was sedated by medication to ease her pain, I saw to it each morning she was as beautiful as she could be. She had on her gold bracelet, her hair was in place, her makeup was done. Although she was near death, it was important to her that no one should see her without her dignity carefully in place.

I remember her mind. As I search for an adjective to characterize her mind, I keep thinking of "hungry." I remember a piece of sculpture she once did in an art class. When we asked her about it, she said that it was her soul. It was made of a gray sculptor's clay, unpainted and unglazed. It was not definable, but somehow bird-like with beak open skyward—thirsty, longing, hungry. The body was small and unimportant in relation to the head and the open, supplicating mouth. "This is my soul," she said. "And the soul is a mind with a mouth." Yes, hungry is the word for my mother-friend's amazing mind.

Her mind seemed to be a living, active thing, separate, yet inseparable from her physical self. If ever there was evidence that there is a soul that has an eternal existence of its own, somehow joined to the mind, her mind was the strong evidence. Her mind would not be silenced. She couldn't turn it off or make it be still. She tried. She would tell it to be still; she would argue with it and command it to lay some knotty question to rest, but it wouldn't obey. Her mind was the only entity I ever knew that could argue her down, silence her objections, and always have the last word. It raised embarrassing issues; it refused to accept placebos. It would not be tranquilized or pacified. Restless as the tides, her mind rolled and heaved, casting perplexities upon the beaches of contemplation.

When the doctor came to deliver the results of the cancer tests, telling her the worst, she considered the prospects of what future she had. We asked her about visitors and projects she wanted to complete. Her instructions were to let any theological or philosophical discussions take place in her presence. And she wanted to see the grandkids and their babies. She bemoaned the fact that the pain was keeping her from concentrating on her reading, and she listed ideas she wanted to think through and write about before her strength ran out.

I thought of a poem she had written long before:

Is This All?

If life has no more purpose
Than to fight to keep alive,
If all there is to living
Is to struggle and to strive

Without a contribution
To some worthwhile total plan,
God went to too much trouble
Just to fashion man.

'Tis sure that there are things of earth
More beautiful than thought—
Things to eat and work to do
And joys that can't be bought.
But even this is not enough
If when we die, we're dead!
There still must be a better use
For this brain in my head.

By the time we learn to do a thing,
That page of life is turned,
And we are left without a cause
To use the thing we've learned.
O what a waste if after all,
No perfect plan comes through—
Man's talents are all scattered
And there is nothing else to do!

I think the God so organized
As the one I've come to know,
Would never stop the story
In the middle of the show!
The truths we learn so slowly
Must not perish with the sun,
And we will learn to use them
When this life's school is done.

We then can think unhampered
By the false, the flaws, the filth
That clog the works so often
And frustrate a world of wealth.
We can soar to heights unfathomed
When from earth's bounds we're free,
For truth will flow unshackled,
And we will finally see!

I am probably only beginning to know now how very right she was. All that we cram into our minds of eternal consequence is not lost and is not wasted. There must be in heaven the meeting of the minds we've been talking about all these years. Her mind was restless to be there; she'd done her homework.

Her hands, her face, her presence, and her mind—these I remember. They are symbols of a working, playing, laughing, scolding, thinking, encouraging, preaching, modeling, praying mother—a friend who stood tall, endured with grit, created out of nothing, refused defeat, served God and the world, and spoke her mind.

I hope I am coming to be a friend like that to my children and grandchildren. I hope that the seeds of friendship she planted are blooming in me on my best days. May her best qualities take root in my children who will one day need to be dependable friends for another generation.

Elizabeth

. . . the calling voice of God is sounding out in the caves and caverns deep beneath the soil of our souls, and it is by obeying this call that we learn who we truly are and what we can become.

Bob Benson

Peggy

A few days ago I went to the funeral of a dear friend. Elizabeth was eighty-nine. She had known me for most of my life, remembering me before I remembered her. My first memories of her began during high school days. She drove me to school and was my confidante during my courtship with a good-looking guy named Bob Benson. When Bob and I married, she was in our corner from day one. We depended on her support and prayers as we began our life in the parsonage. Over the years, she was both friend and mentor as I raised my children and welcomed grandchildren into my life.

As I sat in the service celebrating her homegoing, my mind raced. I remembered our many times together, reconstructing various conversations in my mind. One of her little sayings was, "I don't want to hang around old people." And she didn't! She wanted to "stay up on things" and know what was going on in the world. Bright and thirsty for knowledge, she never made younger women feel insecure. Instead, she had a way of drawing us out, encouraging us to constantly improve ourselves.

One of the delights we shared was an antiques-and-lunch outing. We loved to snoop around in cluttered old shops—the dustier the better—after which we enjoyed good southern cooking. Over lunch we decided what we would do next. I would say to her, "Do you need to get home by a certain time, or do you want to 'do' another shop or two?" Her response was one I now use often myself: "Let's stay longer. I don't have to hurry home to a husband, and there is neither a chick nor child waiting for me!"

Elizabeth didn't always have such a terrific life. Devastating events in her early years might have conquered a less resilient person. But she pulled herself together, picked herself up, dusted herself off, and moved on! She lived out the quote from Bob's book:

"deep in the 'soil of her soul,' she had the drive to be all she could be!" That included using her musical talent as a teacher, investing in real estate, and becoming an amateur historian. She traveled extensively and even managed to earn a bachelor's degree at age sixty-seven.

That day, as the minister began to recall segments of her life, it occurred to me how she had influenced my life. Little did I realize in those early years how her life was speaking to mine. When I became a young widow and a single parent with grown children, deeply saddened by the death of their father, I would draw from her example. In my journal, I wrote:

> She was a person of great integrity,
>   with a sense of style and refinement.
> She was a true southern lady who had
>   courage and dignity in the face of defeat,
> A woman of character with an abiding faith
>   in the deep issues of life.

Elizabeth learned to listen to and obey the voice of the Gardener who worked the soil of her soul. As a result, she became an inspiration to the women whose lives she touched and by her example, taught us to listen for His voice deep within the soil of our own souls.

Sisters—Ever the Best of Friends

She was ten years old when I was born, and I have never known life without her. I don't remember any sibling rivalry, perhaps because she was more my protector than my peer at first. She helped with my bath, fed me when Mother was busy, and showed me off to her friends. When I was bigger she took me places and made sure nobody picked on me.

Gloria

I remember that she took me with her to visit high school when I was four or five years old. I sat in study hall and drew pictures with her colored pencils and circles with her protractor. I thought it was great to move from class to class, and I remember that her teachers made a fuss over me. I got the feeling Evelyn was proud.

I knew I was proud of her! She was the highest scoring forward on the girls' basketball team, and I couldn't wait to grow up to be like her. I liked her brown hair, her saddle shoes, and her boyfriends. I'm not sure they were all that crazy about me, especially when she took me with her on her dates.

"Those guys won't want your little sister tagging along," my mother would tell her.

"If they don't want her around," I'd hear her answer, "they don't want me either." And that was that. I knew I could grab my roller skates and go to the skating rink one more time.

I got quite good at roller skating. But I didn't get good at any other sport. The first day of school was always great for me. My sister's reputation as a crack athlete would always precede me, so when recess came and the kids chose up teams for softball and basketball, I'd always be the first chosen. That was the first day. The second day it was always the same:

"We'll take Sam; you can have Gloria."

"No, that's okay; you can take her. We had her yesterday."

After that I was always the last to be chosen. I resigned myself to the fact that I was uncoordinated and too nearsighted for good depth perception. But I began to show promise in other areas, and it was my sister who always cheered me on.

When I won my first speech contest, she was the first to brag on me. When I was elected president of the student council and tied for valedictorian of my class, she cut the article out of the paper and had it preserved in plastic. When I failed or came home broken-hearted, she was the sympathetic shoulder to cry on; when I succeeded she beamed from ear to ear.

When the calling of my life took me into more public arenas, there was never a shade of jealousy or distance from her. She has loved my husband and my children as her own family and has helped me through pressured times in ways I could never explain.

Her husband Dave has been like a brother to me and has made sacrifices few men would make to keep my sister and me together. When my mother was no longer able to keep up with the schedules of our teenage children while we traveled on weekends, Evelyn and Dave made a complete career change. At a stage when few couples would take such a risk, they moved from Michigan to Indiana to be the stability we could count on.

Our mother's illness and ultimate death from cancer was a bittersweet process we shared together. It made me love Evelyn all the more to share the experience no one can put into words, the experience that left us orphans. Now, we are all that is left of our family of origin. We hold to each other more tightly than ever, treasuring every stolen moment together—each opportunity to share insights from what life is teaching us, each exchange of cute or brilliant antics of our grandchildren. We trade plants from our gardens in the spring and give each other seeds in the fall. We take trips to the nurseries to buy new breeds of geraniums or to find unusual perennials.

In my heart I know the rarest thing we'll ever grow is the deep friendship that will never die with any season. Someone has said, "You can't take it with you," but I am convinced that what my sister and I have grown together is already being transplanted in the perfected Garden of Eden on the sunny banks of Jordan.

Consider the Lilies!

Years ago a friend of mine offered to share her daylilies with me. "It's time to thin them out," she said, "and I want someone to have them who will love them." She obviously didn't know me— know that I didn't know night from day when it came to lilies! "There's nothing prettier than a bed of daylilies," she continued. "They need very little care." That got my attention! Previously, Wayne and I had tried our hand and failed big-time at growing roses. It was a huge relief when we finally turned those pitiful roses over to the aphids, and an even bigger relief when we dug up their scrawny, thorny skeletons and threw them over the hill.

Sue

The fact that I could have beautiful flowers and not have to cater to their every little whim appealed to me. I accepted the daylilies and planted them in a rock garden in sight of our bedroom window. Before I walked away, I shook my finger at them, reminded them they weren't supposed to require much care, explained about the roses, and threatened to throw them over the hill if they didn't behave.

They did as they were told. They bloomed! Summer after summer, I did nothing except admire them from my bedroom window, and wonder why God thought it was worth it to create a flower that bloomed for only one day.

I spent the year after my cancer surgery crawling in and out of bed, either because I was sick as a dog or bone tired from the treatments. Sometimes I was too restless to sleep and too jittery to read, so I propped myself up against pillows and stared into space. When summer came, I stared out of the window at my lilies. Each day I counted the blooms, took note of the lush colors, thought about how handsome they were, and appreciated the fact they were taking care of themselves.

I observed there were whole stalks of buds and that God's plan was that when one conked out—finished for the day—another one (or two) would pop open. As near as I could tell, none of them cheated and hung around longer than they were supposed to.

Why couldn't they stay open longer? I wondered. I pondered the thought that God felt it was worth it to create *one flower* to bloom for *one day*. Even though occasionally my husband or one of my children would look out of the window and comment on the pretty flowers, it occurred to me that many days I was the only person on the face of the earth, in the history of the world, who saw that flower!

Consider the lilies! *That's what I'm doing*, I thought, remembering the words from Scripture. *If a lily is worth it, I'm worth it!* That thought empowered me to go on when it would have been easy to give up.

I survived cancer and several years passed. Just when I thought it would be smooth sailing, I had a much greater crisis to face—the loss of a precious relationship with my beloved daughter. I was in despair! Again I would fling myself on the bed. Again I would stare out of the window into the faces of my exquisite, now much-appreciated, take-care-of-yourselves daylilies. Again, I couldn't sleep. Again I was too strung out to read. Again, I considered the lilies and I copied these words—the words of a favorite song, by Annie Herring—in my journal.

It seems like forever when you're on the down side;
It seems no one's with you walking stride for stride.
You feel through the hard times you're always alone;
And you feel there is nothing you can call your own.

Look, look upon Jesus!
Look upon Him
And consider the lilies
That bloom from within.

They're arrayed with hope
That gives them faith to bloom
Just for a day!
And while they grow they know
They show His heart
In their display!

Look, look upon Jesus!
Look upon Him
And consider the lilies
That bloom from within.

The daylilies are in full bloom again. Again I'm considering the lilies. I'm pondering the same old question: *Why would God make a flower that blooms for only one day?* On the daylily's part, it doesn't seem worth the bother. On God's part, it is—if only to show me, just me, I'm worth it!

Wildflowers

Wildflowers *just come up on their own without being planted. They sprout in unexpected places for unexpected reasons. You don't plant them; you don't cultivate them. They just appear one day, seemingly out of nowhere. You love them, enjoy them, and let them be! They are marvelous and serendipitous surprises of friendship.*

Johnny-jump-ups

Peggy

One of my favorite early spring flowers is the johnny jump-up. It is a first cousin to the pansy. The colors range from deepest purple to palest blue and bright yellows to softest white. They have sweet smiling faces, each with its own personality.

I hurried to plant them one morning before I left town for a weekend of speaking, deciding to put them in clay pots right outside my front door, where they will look up and grin at me as I begin my day.

They remind me that I have some wonderful *jump-up friends* in my life—people who have come into my life over the years at just the exact time I needed to see a friendly, smiling face. These folks are not an everyday part of my life on a consistent basis; I think of them as my *cheering section*. They are people who believe in me and have let me know it in many ways. They have supervised the care and feeding of my children when I was in the hospital, and all the many years Bob was ill. Once, when he was in intensive care and the prognosis was pretty grim, they orchestrated the move from our home in the country to a small, temporary condo. What a chore it was to pack the furnishings, bric-a-brac, and boxes of memories that represented twenty years of our lives. These same people gave me comfort when my mom died and are still giving me the courage I need as I care for my father. They are quick to send a note of encouragement, make a phone call, or surprise me with a birthday gift. What a tremendous rescue team I have!

Each morning, the sweet smiling faces of the small flowers look up at me as they settle their roots into the earth. I smile back as I see in them the faces of my "jump-up" friends: Judy, Martha, and Connie. Betty, Joy, and Joann. Peggy, Beverly, Jane, and Elane. Wilma, Pat, and Nita. Trish, Betty, Eunice, and Jan. The list goes on and on!

During the days of spring, as I walk into my garden and think and pray about my life—where I've been and where I might be next—I smile to myself and remember, and I thank God for Johnny-jump-ups!

My Unlikely Friend

We should never have been friends. I was deeply rooted in the Midwest; she had grown up in San Francisco and lived in Boulder, Colorado, when I met her. I was married to my husband of thirty years and had three grown children and a grandchild; she had been divorced, remarried, then prematurely widowed. I was a Protestant evangelical Christian, she was a Buddhist convert from a Catholic/Jewish home. My conservative parents had been pastors of small churches all my life; her liberal parents were both well-known journalists. My political leanings were Republican; hers were a little left of Democrat. I tended to think patriotic citizens served in the armed forces in times of national conflict; she had gone to Canada with her husband because they both thought the Vietnam war was illegal and immoral and believed that caring citizens should refuse to support it. I gave birth to my children in a hospital; her husband had helped deliver her babies in a remote area without modern facilities or medical care.

I met her when I was doing research for my master's thesis in American Literature. I was working on creating a musical stage play based on one of John Steinbeck's earliest novels. I had applied for and received a grant from the university where I studied to visit the sights that were the setting for the novel and to interview as many people as I could who could shed light on this work and its history. Since Nancy had been the wife of John Steinbeck's oldest son, John IV, she was one of the people I interviewed during this process.

At first I was careful to keep our conversations on a purely academic level. She was very intimately involved in the work I was researching and was a wealth of helpful information. The more I talked with her, the more I knew there was something special about her—a sort of spiritual quality—that drew me to her. I loved her honest no-nonsense way of stripping life to its bare essentials. I liked her direct answers and her easy way of relating to everyone without pretense. I admired her bright mind and quick wit.

As we became better acquainted, I found it refreshing to have someone in my life that knew or cared nothing about my

Gloria

101

accomplishments or reputation except as a legitimate scholar and as a human being. The more we talked together about the literature, the more we ended up talking about life and what it was supposed to be about. Little by little we began to trust each other with access into guarded areas of our lives. What we were learning was that our trust was developing from a shared honesty about what experience had taught us.

I knew, of course, that eventually such discussions would lead to the question of the source of life and our relationship with God. But I wanted that to come naturally, and I wanted to earn the right to talk about spiritual things by having these discussions based on mutual trust and respect.

In the meantime, God saw to it that Nancy was not the only Buddhist in my life, and I began reading a lot about Zen Buddhism to learn what common ground of truth we shared and where the points of departure actually were. I didn't want to be guilty of a prejudice based on ignorance and suspicion. I wanted to trust the truth that God had built into the universe and to accept the fact that I and those in my comfort zone had no special corner on what God had been revealing to mankind for centuries—that which was ultimately expressed in Jesus Christ.

I deeply believed that anyone who honestly was hungering and thirsting for truth would be filled, and that her quest would lead eventually to the living, walking Truth. There was an openness on her part too, and she eventually asked what I did as a vocation, because she had learned I was a writer and lyricist.

"What kind of lyrics do you write?" she asked me. "What sorts of books?"

Carefully, I sent her a few things I had written and prayed that she was ready. Her response told me that I had found a very special flower in the garden of friendship. She accepted what I did as a part of who I was. She also told me more about herself, her history, her pilgrimage, and her aspirations.

To my surprise she decided to come to a retreat where I was speaking. She talked openly about what I had to say and shared questions and observations about life from her perspective. I learned about the circumstances that had made her lose faith in organized religion, and with that, I found that what had survived in spite of it all was a deep, spiritual hunger and a knowing that God had never left her, even in the times when it was hardest for her to find a valid expression of God in those who claimed to represent Him.

Her openness and vulnerability gave me permission to express my own questions and doubts and to confide in her how I had found Jesus Christ to be the reality of my life. I was freed to articulate that I had found in Him, not a religion or a creed, but a living vital force called the Holy Spirit that could infuse a person with the courage to risk and the power to walk the faith-life path I had found to be the great adventure.

My friendship with Nancy has taught me many things. I have learned that it isn't necessary to resolve all differences for two people to be friends. I have learned that the space and air between two people are as important to a relationship as the times of unity and closeness. Nancy has made me believe more than ever that life is a process and that each of life's experiences—the pain, the glory, the heartaches, and the triumphs—are all part of soul growth. To God, process is not a means to a goal. Process is the goal of life that keeps us moving closer, always closer to an intimate friendship with Him.

Watching Nancy relate to her two young adult children, Megan and Michael, who are about the ages of our Amy and Benjamin, has made me a better mother. I've observed that she spends a lot more time delighting in where they are in their lives—celebrating the gift of each moment with them—than she spends worrying about where they are going. She seems to live out a belief that if each moment is embraced and lived to the maximum of its potential, the future will take care of itself.

I have a feeling Jesus would say it like this:

> *Give your entire attention to what God is doing right now, and don't get worked up about what may not happen tomorrow. God will help you deal with whatever hard things come up when the time comes.*
>
> *Walk into the fields and look at the wildflowers . . . most of them never are seen, don't you think He'll attend to you, take pride in you, do His best for you?*
>
> *What I'm trying to do here is to get you to relax, not be so preoccupied with getting so you can respond to God's giving. . . . The Father wants to give you the very kingdom itself!* Matt. 6:34; Luke 12:27–28, 30 THE MESSAGE

A Crocus! . . . It Is Spring!

Daffodils and tulips
Impatient underground
When March sent up a crocus
To take a look around.
Said the crocus, "It is winter!
There's frost on everything!"
But a passerby who saw her said,
"A crocus! It is Spring!"

Author unknown

Daffodils and tulips may be the first to tenuously poke their impatient green noses out to test the spring temperatures, but those crusty crocuses are the real movers and shakers. With wild abandonment, they thrust their animated antennae into a frigid, unfriendly world and announce with cheerful exuberance, "Ready or not, here comes spring!"

My friend Lynn is a crocus! She spreads exuberance like soft, fresh peanut butter on thick-sliced bread. Her zest for life is palpable. I am at the age where I sometimes feel old and dull and eaten up with self-pity—but never in her presence! There is enthusiastic welcome in her smile, her voice, and often, her hug. I never feel that I am just one more interruption in her day, and as a busy professional writer and musician and a mother of three, she has a zillion!

Though she is eighteen years my junior, we discovered early in our relationship that we shared one of the great secrets of the universe: If you think you can—you probably can!

As young teenagers, nearly a generation apart, we were doers. Our boot camps were a combination of family and church, separated by hundreds of miles—hers, a church in a small Alabama town; mine, my father's church in northern Michigan. In each context, there was always a job to do, and precious few willing or available to accept the challenge, so we stepped confidently up to the plate and said with conviction, "I can do that!" And we did.

Years later, as part of a newly formed congregation in Nashville, already numbering a thousand, I watched this young woman, fresh out of graduate school, stand before a choir of forty adults twice her age. She was up there, waving her arms, acting as if she knew exactly what she was doing. She did!

Almost at first meeting, Lynn and I experienced a dynamic bonding in our shared life perspective. We saw in each other qualities we had come to treasure for ourselves—openness, vulnerability, enthusiasm for a task, and an innate self-confidence that probably often exceeded our abilities. The latter never stopped us. We forged ahead—as we have with a friendship in which we have rarely stopped to notice the difference in our ages and stages in life, in our geo-cultural backgrounds or our body types: she's a Miss Alabama runner-up; my body would be less likely to impress a beauty pageant judge! Okay, a *lot* less likely! Let's get back to Lynn being a crocus—and how joyed I am every time she springs into my day!

Just when the green of spring seems forever beyond reach . . . a bud appears!

(I Hate to Admit It, but ...)
I Was Wrong!

I never judge a person unless I have to. I say that to my friends and they know I'm trying to be funny. They also know the truth—that I *am* often judgmental, that I'm prone to stereotype a person before she has a chance to open her mouth. A librarian? *Bor–ring*. A musician? *Flaky, unpredictable*. An earring in his ear? *Well, you know what I think about that!* She's a blonde? *Probably dumb as a wall*. I meet 'em, categorize 'em, and stuff 'em into a box—to stay. I'm often very wrong! My sister-in-law, a librarian, is one of the most interesting conversationalists I know, and of my many musician acquaintances, only a handful are flaky, and wait . . . I myself am a blonde! Not a blonde by God's design—He Himself has forgotten the true color—but nevertheless a blonde.

Rick was one of those people about whom I was very wrong. I not only judged him, subconsciously, I'm sure I wrote him off as someone with whom I would have little in common. Rick is my daughter's brother-in-law, and I met him during the festivities surrounding her marriage to Barry.

I'm sure my brain played connect the dots where Rick was concerned: big, handsome, wavy blonde hair (dare I say *hunk?*) with ability to weave the sports scores into any and all conversations. He had a thick neck (meaning he participated in sports at some time in his life), and before I knew it—I admit it—I thought, *Thick neck! Thick brain!*

Yes, I'm out of my mind with embarrassment, but it's true. And I can hear what my friends are saying behind my back, "Can you believe she said that? After all, she herself is no Einstein!" I can even hear the voice of my dear mother coming to me from the grave: "Looks to me like the pot is calling the kettle black."

My first book, which was about surviving breast cancer with one's sense of humor and sexuality intact, made the rounds of Dana's new family. Bonnie, Dana's mother-in-law and administrative assistant to one of the world's top cancer researchers, became my best PR person. She not only recommended my book but bought several copies to pass around to her friends and relatives. I had heard from several of them, and they had been effusive in their compliments.

Every first-time author loves having her book praised. Perhaps after the tenth or twelfth book, compliments become old hat, but when you're a new writer, you soak them up like a sponge.

My all-time favorite fan letter is from Rick. Yes, *that* Rick! The one with whom I supposedly had nothing in common.

It arrived in a thick envelope with my name and address printed across the front. I sat down in the big chair by the window, ran my fingernail across the seal, and pulled out a thick wad of yellow legal paper, folded askew, looking as though perhaps the writer was afraid he might change his mind about mailing it.

I began to read. After a few pages, I was sobbing. Soon the tears were dripping off my chin and splatting across the naked thoughts scrawled between the narrow blue lines. These were the words of a man who had buried his pain so far beneath the skin that once unleashed, it seemed to gush from every pore of his body.

"I'm home today because of snow," he wrote. (He is a teacher and coach.) "It's a good day to stay home and read books." He explained that Becky, his wife, had been reading my book and he thought he would glance through it. "I couldn't put it down," he said, "and before I knew it, I had finished it. I wanted to share my thoughts with you if you don't mind. I feel I know you well," he wrote, and then he began a story that went something like this:

November 1, 1967, as I walked into our apartment in Lewisburg, Ohio, I noticed two complete strangers, sitting in the living room. Dave, my fifteen-year-old brother, was in the kitchen, so I kept walking toward him and asked what was going on. He told me that Mom had gone to the hospital for some tests and they had decided to keep her there. The two strangers were the superintendent of a children's home and his social worker. My first reaction was that of fear, and I guess I did what any thirteen-year-old kid might do. I took off running from the apartment, but they caught me later that night with the help of the police.

I was angry! Angry that my father had died in a car accident when I was four! Angry that Mom's family, her brother and parents, had died before I ever got to know them! Angry that her live-in, jerk boyfriend had disappeared and left her with all the bills. There were five of us, and Mom was doing her best to raise us without the help of welfare.

For the next three weeks, we were stuck in the children's home until Mom was able to come home at Thanksgiving. I had no idea what was wrong with her until a nurse stopped by to change her bandage. I walked into the bedroom just as she had the dressing off, and I could see that one breast had been removed. I was devastated. Mom must have seen the feeling in my face because she called me over and told me that everything would be okay. I never could understand why she had to go back to the hospital and why we had to go back to the children's home. She came home again at Christmas but was not very well, and her other breast was gone.

In March I got off the bus from school, and Pop Swank, the superintendent, met us on the porch and told us Mom had died. I cried then but never again. Not throughout the viewing, not during the funeral, not at the reception. No tears. None at all, and after the funeral I couldn't speak for about a month.

I noted that Rick's writing style was changing to that of a bewildered little boy rather than that of a grown man. He stopped often to apologize for his spelling, sentence structure, and handwriting.

Rick told me that my book had helped him understand what his mother had gone through "as a woman who was losing part of her womanhood." He explained that for the first time, he could feel her fear. "What hurts most is to know that my mother had to go through that alone."

Several times Rick referred to specifics from my story, such as my experience with the man who was married to my mother and how he kept me away from her during the months before her death. "God! How I understood that," Rick said. "I, too, missed having the chance to be with my mom when she needed me most. (Excuse me—I need to cry some.)"

Rick needed to cry some and so did I. I needed to cry, because for a moment, I was Rick's mother and in that role, I could see how I would be torn between two possibilities: that of distancing myself from my child, thus creating a barrier that would ease his—and my own—pain; or gathering him close and keeping him by my side to witness and document my inevitable, slow, and horrendous demise.

The decision, in fact, was probably made by other people—people in white coats with dangling stethoscopes and the others from the children's home who felt they had the best interests of the children in mind.

Rick continued: "I'm back after coffee and a cookie. Thanks for waiting. Becky doesn't know all the tears I've shed in this reading. Thank you for helping me understand the pain my mother must have been experiencing."

In my book, I had written my memories of Christmas—the Christmas I thought would be my last—and it prompted Rick to remember his mother's last Christmas. "She left us a trillion pictures," he continued. "I'm not crazy, but I put my mom's face on you when you described your times with your friends and family." Then he described in great detail his own outings with his mother—how she would fry chicken for a picnic and how they loved to fish, play basketball, and romp in the water.

"I hardly know you, and look at all the writing," he continued. "Thank you for giving me a glimpse of what my mother must have gone through and helping me remember what she was like. I wish she could still be here to love me and my children. Mom loved kids and I know she would spoil mine."

His writing now seemed to change again as he described the emotional and spiritual growth he had experienced since his marriage. The letter took on the characteristics of a man, secure and happy in his world. It occurred to me he had confronted the terrible dragons synonymous with caring deeply, had bravely made the choice, and that it was well worth the risks!

"Enough is enough!" proclaimed the last paragraph of this very long letter. "Thanks for helping me with the feelings I needed to feel. The tears have come often! It was good to feel close to my mom again after all these years. Thank you sincerely! Your friend, Rick."

Rick, *my friend!* I'm humbled by the fact of it.

Not long ago our phone rang. It was Rick. He was passing through town headed for a missions trip with three members of his church youth group and wondered if I could recommend a motel. *It just happened* I had a big pot of soup cooking, and *it just happened* I had made a big pan of brownies, and *it just happened* that Rick couldn't resist my invitation to bring his friends to spend the night.

We stayed up late and talked and laughed and shared stories. To say we had a wonderful time is an understatement.

Now when our families get together for Thanksgiving and other occasions, I see Rick in a new light. I see a sensitive husband and a loving, involved father. I see a you-can-count-on-me churchman and community leader. I feel proud when I hear about his successes, including the unique sports program he has created at the school where he teaches.

I love walking through the woods with Rick and Becky and their children and crawling into the closet to see the latest litter of kittens. I love the teasing—the back and forth bantering that takes place between us. Recently, another envelope arrived from Rick, following a phone call I'd made asking him for permission to share this story. This time the envelope held a full-page magazine photo of an airbrushed-perfect man, elegantly stretched out on a chaise couch. Pasted over the face was Rick's face and the note attached said, "You will probably need a picture of me for the book. I just wanted to accommodate. Love, Rick."

Not long ago when Dana and Barry were home, we looked through the wedding pictures and video. There was Rick. For me, it was as though a spotlight—or maybe a halo—enhanced his image. There was Rick shooting video. There was Rick telling funny stories at the rehearsal dinner. There was Rick performing the duties of a groomsman. Hugging! Smiling! Smiling? Funny, I never noticed that at the time.

Celebrations of Friendship ...
Enjoying the Garden

A bountiful garden—and a life, open and receptive to friendship—both are sanctuaries for all seasons, welcoming all kinds of plants and producing wonderful results: annuals for color and pizzazz; shade plants for peace, tranquillity, and contemplation; perennials for long-enduring, history-sharing beauty; and wildflowers for spontaneity, carefree celebration, and surprise. Friends, like those lovingly characterized in this book, are a bouquet of flowers arranged in a lovely vase. The sum of them brings to our lives a glorious melange of color, texture, and form, at once reminding us of our roots, enriching our present, and giving purpose to our future.

Perfect note to a friend: "I thank God for the surprise of you in my life!"

Indiana Weekend

A perfect Indiana summer weekend at the Gaithers was something the "Nashville Gang" had all looked forward to for months: Bob, Joy, their children Kristen and Shana; Carlana and her daughter Angela; Wayne, me, and our daughter Mindy. We couldn't wait to get there!

As far as we were concerned, our intentions might as well have been chiseled in stone. We had a plan and we intended to keep it! We would be lying by the pool, playing tennis, lying by the pool, swimming, lying by the pool, stuffing ourselves with great food, and lying by the pool.

We would discuss! We would grapple! We would philosophize! Not a topic or idea would be off-limits. Anything could be discussed —poked, prodded, turned inside-out-and-back-again discussed!

I'm sorry to say, however, that after this weekend, there would be something that couldn't be discussed—would henceforth be mentioned only in whispers with fear and trepidation.

We arrived late Thursday night, and after brief hellos, fell into our beds. The hoped-for luxury of sleeping late the next morning was shattered by a loud voice and an even louder slamming door.

"You guys awake?" We pulled the pillows over our heads and tried to ignore Bill's presence at the bedroom door. "If we weren't, we are now," Wayne growled. For the next few minutes Bill danced from bedroom to bedroom, proclaiming the weather to be perfect, preaching his usual sermon on the virtues of Indiana, and chastising us for our slovenly sleep habits. At last he retreated, urging us to hurry, get dressed, and come over to the house. "Coffee's on. Gloria's fixin' breakfast." The door slammed behind him.

We ate our scrumptious country breakfast dressed in our cover-ups with bathing suits beneath, knowing we'd move from the kitchen to the pool before the morning was over, taking our conversation with us.

Our children had been swimming for a couple of hours by the time we spread our towels and staked our territory by the pool. We moved easily from subject to subject, barely finishing one topic before another was begun. Sometimes the men would slip into the water to talk about whatever it is men talk about. Other times we women would monopolize the pool, bedding down on floaters and attaching ourselves to each other's mattresses like a large pinwheel, to accommodate our girl talk.

"This is the life!" Our happy proclamations filled the air. "I could live like this!" And, we kept reminding ourselves, the weekend had just begun.

The children hung around awhile listening to adult conversation. None of us can remember a time, before or since, when this particular bunch of kids behaved this way. "We don't know what to do," they whined. "We're bored." Joy excused their behavior by pointing out how our children had grown and how the age gap had widened. Suzanne was beginning to look and act like a young woman, and Shana, Amy, and Mindy weren't far behind (our Dana was back in Nashville working a summer job). Angela and Benjy must have been seven or eight at the time, and Kristen a couple of years younger. Even with the age differences, our kids still wanted to be together.

What do you mean you have nothing to do? The retort was on the tip of my tongue—the tongue I was biting! Didn't these kids know about child labor in Latin America? Did they have any idea how lucky they were? I could sense the others were as annoyed as I; that is, except for Gloria, who always seemed to be in tune with the children's needs. Sure enough she had a suggestion. "Why don't you go upstairs to the playroom and write a movie? Give everyone a part. Practice it and tomorrow you can videotape it with the new camera. We'll help you if you need us." That last comment caused Bob to groan and Carlana to roll her eyes heavenward. *In your dreams,* I thought as I rolled over and pretended to nap. The children disappeared and our day was once again perfect—exactly what we had envisioned.

That evening as we ate our picnic dinner, the kids announced that early the next morning the filming of *The Great Kidnaping Caper* would begin. Shana and Suzanne had script in hand; they had worked all day and were so excited they literally danced, out-shouting each other with an animated description of the upcoming production. Into the cacophony of their excitement we inserted loud exclamations of encouragement. That's nice! . . . wonderful! . . . sounds great! . . . good idea!

As the storyline unfolded, we swallowed our encouraging words along with the potato salad. Unfortunately we, the adults, had been chosen for starring roles in this epic of Hollywood proportions. Had they not been so caught up in their own genius, they surely would have noticed our eyes glazing over. This was the last thing, *the very last thing,* we wanted to do—ruin a precious day by playing with the kids.

Being the supportive parents we were, though, we jumped in with what could best be described as a let's-get-this-thing-over-with kind of enthusiasm, and surprisingly it wasn't long until all of us were into it. Really into it! Not only that, the next morning we were shouting orders, making script changes, and offering ideas for costumes. Someone suggested an additional character—preferably an actress who owned a gun. Angela and Benjy were ordered to run across the bridge to get Grandma Honeysickle. (That's what the kids called Dorothy Sickal, Gloria's mother.)

Tell her to bring her big cowboy hat and her gun," Gloria shouted after them. "Amy and Mindy, (costume department) go find that sheriff's badge in the toy box," she ordered. By this time Gloria had designated herself cameraperson.

Scene one takes place in the living room of the guest house where two little children (Benjy and Angela) are playing quietly on the floor. Their mother (Carlana) is ironing; their father (Bill) is reading the paper. A quarrel breaks out between the parents and develops into a full-blown, name-calling, arm-flailing, screaming match. (No doubt our children had witnessed this behavior on TV. No one dared ask.)

Before long the children decide to run away from home. The parents soon realize they are missing and call the police, played by Joy and me, both of us dressed in bright police-blue bathing suits. (Surely a precursor to TV's *Baywatch*.) The costume department provided badges—large stars made of cardboard and aluminum foil—and plastic billy clubs from the toy box. Metal mixing bowls from Gloria's kitchen were plunked upside down on our heads. At this point in time, before their characters were introduced, Suzanne, Shana, Amy, and Mindy are acting as script girls, costume department, grips, and what-have-you. Wayne and Bob, the two who groaned loudest when the plan was presented, are now overpowering everyone with script changes and directions.

Suddenly the scene shifts outdoors and Officers Joy and Sue call on Sheriff Honeysickle to assist! The camera flashes back and forth from the frightened children lost in the woods to the faces of the anguished parents. The children finally crumble to the ground and sob loudly. Then Angela dramatically raises her head, smiles, and points off in the distance to a charming playhouse, a haven in the strange woods. But the hope in the children's faces is immediately dashed when they realize that two thugs, Rosco and Bucko (Bob and Wayne), are hiding out there with the loot from a bank robbery. Rosco and Bucko know a good thing when they see it, grab the kids, and, in barely understandable "thug talk," issue a ransom demand in exchange for the kids' return. They tie up the kids and wait for the payoff, whiling away their time gambling with jumbo dinosaur cards designed for four-year-olds. "Aay! Bucko! Trade you a brontosaur for a tyrannosaur."

I'm not just saying this because I was in it, but the next scene where the law swings into action was one of the finest moments in motion picture history. It was pure magic! You've watched the technique used in every cops-'n-robbers movie you've ever seen. The cameraperson is at the bottom of a hill. (This time it's Gloria, lying on her back on the ground.) The law enforcement officers march over the horizon, down the hill, and past the camera. In a Hollywood production you can count on a dramatic sound track. In our case Wayne, Bob, and Bill make *Dragnet*-like sound effects with their mouths as Joy, Grandma Honeysickle, and I march over the hill, shoulder to shoulder, billy clubs swinging, and past the camera. It was spectacular!

I'd like to be able to tell you every detail from here on—the capture and imprisonment of the thugs, the return of the children, the happy-ever-after family—but the details are fuzzy in my memory. I *do* remember that Rosco and Bucko were captured and thrown into jail, but that's about it.

Why don't I remember more, considering we captured it all on tape? The video, I'm sorry to say, no longer exists. I'm not one to name names, and heaven forbid I should cast blame, but I can say that *someone* recorded an Indiana Pacers game over our masterpiece. End of story!

Since that summer weekend many years ago, the "Nashville Gang" has had some great times together. We've played tennis, lazed around the pool, stuffed ourselves with good food, grappled with great ideas, and philosophized about everything and anything. We discuss any subject. Well, almost any subject!

There is one subject, a walk-on-eggshells-off-limits-don't-mention-it topic—*The Great Kidnapping Caper* video! On the few occasions when someone has dared bring it up, nostrils have flared and the subject has been dropped like the hot potato it is.

I've often wondered what would happen if the tape showed up again. What if it had been there all along, simply mislabeled? What if tonight we could all sit down and watch it?

The truth is, I think we would all be disappointed. Disappointed to find out we weren't the brilliant actors we thought we were, that our children weren't nearly as cute as we'd imagined, and that it wasn't the magnificent production we remember. I think we would be sadly disappointed!

I'm not sure I want any of this story to get back to the Indiana Pacers fan (whose nostrils flare). I especially would not want this next revelation made known to him. Sometimes what's filed in our memories is better—much better!—than what has taken place in real life. Perhaps this is one of those times.

The Garden Path

If we find we are too busy for friends, we must conclude we are too busy. Life is a façade if it speeds past the lasting in pursuit of the transient. The garden path is something we have to plan and maintain. It must give us joy to create it, satisfaction to sustain it, and delight to walk it. How sad it would be to grow a friendship that we're too busy to enjoy! Garden paths are made and walked on purpose; we must choose to be there. The more we make time for enjoying friendships in the summer of life when we are the busiest, the more familiar and dear the garden path will be in the autumn of life, and the more natural it will be for our feet to take us there. A well-worn path is the lovely habit of friendship.

And Miss the Joy . . .

It's one of those days when it seems everything needs to be done at once. The house needs cleaning, laundry needs to be done, I have a luncheon engagement, the lawn is knee-high, the petunias need pinching, and this is the last day to get sheets at the Dillard's linen sale. There's that baby shower tomorrow night for which I have yet to buy a gift, and I told Minnie three days ago I'd call her back and haven't had a spare moment since. I hope it wasn't something important. I try to swallow the lump in my throat.

Sometimes the very desire for action leads to the neglect of action. We're so busy searching for the perfect opportunity, the most effective method, the favorable moment—so intent are we on improving on God's timing—that we not only disqualify ourselves for the mission and miss the joy, but an urgent need is left unanswered—forever.

I have often experienced the pull of an inner voice, urging me to call a friend who is in need. Invariably, I address that urge by checking my watch to see if the time is appropriate—or by mentally reprioritizing my schedule to accommodate a more convenient arrangement.

"That will be a better listening time," I reason. "The children will be in bed."

Born of genuine concern for my friend, my determination to provide the most propitious response thwarts the entire effort. The perfect moment never arrives; there is never a convenient time.

When my friend most needed simply to hear a reassuring voice, I wasn't available. I was busy rearranging God's schedule. I can still feel the lump in my throat . . .

The spirit of the garden is the spirit of giving. It gives in all seasons. Even when it appears dead, deep in the heart of its soil, it is preparing to deliver once again in abundance and variety.

We have friendships like that—friendships which, once nurtured, are now neglected. In the barren season, they go on giving. Where there is love, life renews itself with absolute certainty! Amazing!

A Boat Trip with Girlfriends

Mmmm . . . So good to get away from the everyday of life. Perfect solitude . . . Time to reflect, read, write . . . and pray.

God has manifest Himself in breathtaking sunsets . . . and a dancing porpoise show: "Together now, up and out of the water . . . smile and dive," say the porpoise . . . "under the boat and out. . . . higher this time. . . . They love us!"

Sue

Today we saw a rainbow . . . a complete rainbow. We considered sailing off to find the pot of gold. But whatever would we do with a pot of gold? . . . And who would believe our story?

Tonight we made up silly songs and poetry, joint venturing one about the captain of our ship. . . . We are silly beyond words.

To think we almost didn't come. . . ."Too busy," we said. Busy doing what? It slips my mind just now.

Before one of our "girls only" trips, we are the epitome of wife-liness, with a lot of let-me-cook-your-favorite-meal-sweetheart-let's-just-spend-the-evening-watching-one-of-those-exciting-football-games-on-TV-baby, honey talk.

Big Papa

Recently my children and their mates and a rather large assortment of grandchildren, along with my sister, Bo, made the trip across town to worship with my dad. He has been the organist at Memorial Lutheran Church for almost forty years. The occasion was especially meaningful, for it was the last regular service that Big Papa, as he is

known by most people, would be playing. All those years, through snowstorms and heat waves and failing health, he had been faithful to this small community of believers.

In typical fashion, I was late! Rushing quickly into the sanctuary, my heart was flooded with memories of stories Dad had told me about his friends at church: the times he had been called to play for baptisms, weddings, funerals, church suppers and parties, not to mention regular services and special holy days. His life was so woven into the fabric of this close-knit family of God's people, I wondered if they could possibly know how much they meant to him—especially this morning as he prepared to leave his post forever.

When I looked up into the balcony, toward the organ, there he sat, grinning his warm sly grin. My daddy is a small, dapper fellow with lots of facial hair, a full mustache, a beard, and a fringe of white hair all the way around his head, but not much left on top. He has a potbelly, twinkling eyes, and a booming voice that causes the walls to vibrate when he talks. My husband said Big Papa probably learned to whisper in a sawmill! This morning, as every Sunday morning, he had on his lovely white choir robe, shirred from the yoke at the shoulders, and over the robe lay his lovely silver cross on a black ribbon. I didn't like to think that I would never see him in this robe again. It occurred to me how regal and angelic he looked as he set about doing his task. Many Sundays he had played when his load was heavy and his heart was broken. On this day, he played with all the gusto an eighty-two-year-old man could muster.

When the worship service ended, my children hurried to tell me what I had missed by being late. Dad had come out of the choir room door at the front of the sanctuary and started down the aisle toward the back of the sanctuary and the balcony where the organ is housed. To his surprise and delight, he saw his grandchildren and great-grandchildren lining the pews, waiting for church to begin. Excited to see them he began to smile and hug and kiss the children. Then he proceeded up the aisle toward the back of the church. As he did, one by one, parishioners got up from their pews and rushed to his side. Soon they were standing in line—waiting with hugs and smiles, affirmation and gratitude for a job well done. There was laughter and tears and words of encouragement. His eyes brimming, Dad turned to the pastor who was left standing at the pulpit, and said, "You will have to give me a moment, Pastor. I have to have my hugs. This is what keeps me going."

This was a day my dad will remember until his memory is gone. Even then, if you put your ear up close to his heart, you might hear a quiet little melody . . . maybe his favorite:

> Fear not, I am with thee, oh be not dismayed
>> For I am thy God, I will still give thee aid.
> I'll strengthen thee, help thee, and cause thee to stand
>> Upheld by My gracious, omnipotent hand.

As I write of this special day in the life of my father, I can't help thinking of the lessons I've learned from my garden: to pay attention, to care for and cultivate, to protect and rescue from the blast of winter and the drought of summer. Many Sundays, it would have been easier for Dad to stay at home, but like the gardener who pays attention to his plot of earth, Dad was faithful! Isn't that like the heavenly Father? So generously faithful, He pays attention to our needs. He loves us so much He sends us the rain and the sun and, in due time, harvest.

(On July 15, 1997, Big Papa met the Master Gardener at heaven's gate.)

Notes to Joy from Gloria

Summer, 1982 (during the time of Bob's heart attack and bypass surgery)

Dear Joy,

I lift you up as you learn the path in this new, uncharted territory. I hope it brings you joy to know that although you walk uniquely, you do not walk alone. You are so loved.

Gloria

Joy,

I am giving thanks today for friendship and love—specifically for yours and Bob's friendship and love—and praising God for the opportunity to lift and love you at this time in your lives. Even when you are too tired or preoccupied to pray, please lie back in the knowing that the praying is being done by us who love and treasure you so.

Gloria

Joy,

Hope is never a victim of circumstance, but is firmly rooted in "forever." It is not a fragile, mystical illusion, but a reality with guts and muscle.

We send and share His Hope. I love you.

Gloria

Joy,

Small reminders continue to assure us that God is there and that He is at work in the smallest detail of our days.

I saw a mountain today and knew that to reach the summit, it must be climbed. We climb with you your mountain.

Love,
Gloria

The Garden Bench

Friendships and gardens need to be absorbed, enjoyed, and appreciated if they are to fill our hearts with joy. We all need stopping places where we can sit under a tree, smell the roses, eat an apple, and tell stories to the children. Place many benches in the garden of friendship: a cup of coffee, a morning walk, a meeting place, a shopping trip, a shared time of prayer.

So I Won't Forget . . .

from Gloria's Journal, January 4, 1986

This day is for silence. So many voices call to me, "No, there is no time! You must spend this day doing!"

But I know that my "doing" is of dwindling value when there is no space for silence. Speaking is no good without first listening to what was spoken into the space of the Beginning. Words are drained of their meaning when there is no focus on the Word that is, that was in the space of the first silence, quiet yet insistent.

And how can I start a new year without attention to silence and an inward journey into space—the space within myself, the space without? It is space that traces around me, like a child traces around her hand on a clean page of paper, separating what is me from the throng of other souls on this crowded earth. Without the space, I would blend into the masses and, in time, forget that I am.

"Once the realization is accepted that even between the closest human beings infinite distances continue to exist, a wonderful living side-by-side can grow up if they succeed in loving the distance which makes it possible for each to see the other whole against the sky."

from *Letters to a Young Poet* by Rainer Mario Rilke, translated by Stephen Mitchell.

Friends in the Pew

You wouldn't have much of a church if every member were like me. It takes dependable people to keep a church going—teaching Sunday school, singing in the choir, working in the nursery—and I may as well tell you here and now, I'm not very dependable. I'm absent from church at least a third of the time because of my travel schedule. I tell the pastor I'm waiting for a job that comes with no responsibility but a lot of glory. He's looking.

Sue

Anyone who has met our pastor thinks of him as a friend. He has an unusual way of tuning in and finding a way to "connect" with everyone he meets. Several years ago he and I "connected" when we acted opposite each other in a Christmas play. I played the role of a sour, self-righteous, opinionated old lady named Edna Puckett, and the pastor played himself. Edna tells the pastor *her* spiritual gift is the gift of "criticism" and throughout the play makes nasty jabs at him under the pretense of trying to help:

"Preacher, people like the beginnings of your sermons and they like the endings of your sermons. We just wish you'd get the two closer together." "I have just three words to say about your sermons, preacher, *Lo–ooo–ong!*"

These are Edna's comments, not mine! It is I, however, who shakes the pastor's hand on Sunday morning, and I'm the one who has to be ready for his exit poll question: "So what would Aunt Edna have to say about today's sermon?"

"She'd say her hypoglycemia was acting up, and if you go that long again, preacher, you'd better stuff the bulletins with Tootsie Rolls and oyster crackers."

Occasionally Edna will write the pastor a letter with a theological brainteaser: "Preacher, do you think all depravity is *total* depravity? Is there such a thing as *partial* depravity?" She also confesses to pinching the legs of the people who pass by her in the pew.

I have many church friends. There are certain people that I simply must *see*—get my hands on. I need a touch, a handshake, a hug, or all of the above. If I don't get them, I feel as if I haven't been to church.

My eyes scan the audience to find Mr. Tom. We call him that because he's a scoutmaster and that's what the kids call him. He's tall and easy to spot. Mr. Tom went beyond the call of duty once when we had a family crisis. It's something we'll never forget.

Then there is Helen, who greets me the same way each time I see her: "You're so beautiful." Is it any wonder I practically jump the pews to get to her? Once right out of the blue, she gave me a beautiful dress—a to-die-for-movie-star dress—that she couldn't wear anymore.

I have a number of friends in the choir, and before we moved into the new sanctuary, when the seats weren't so far back, I enjoyed making faces and crossing my eyes, knowing I could make Sue Even-wel laugh. Lynn and I actually have an unspoken eye-language. When Nancy is a worship leader, I feel as proud as though she were my own daughter.

Our minister of music, John, and his wife, Marty, are what I call "bandwagon" friends. They are willing to drop everything to help you get a job done. They can take any idea and make it better—and not just in theory. They are ready to swing from ladders to help decorate or to get their hands dirty in the kitchen. We rarely have time to exchange words on Sunday morning, but often I feel a hand on my arm or a kiss on my cheek, as one or the other whooshes by.

Then there is Olivia. In our Presbyterian church we don't dance in the aisles, but if we did, Olivia would lead the pack. She can barely contain herself. I hug her every chance I get, in the hopes that some of the joy she experiences in worship will rub off on me.

Our church is divided into small fellowship groups that meet at various times during the week. Ours meets every Sunday evening and I can assure you we're faithful to Scripture. You know the verse—the one that says, "Where two or three are gathered in My name, someone will bring a casserole! And appetizers! And salad! And vegetables! And a couple of different desserts!" In our case, since we never check with one another, it could be eight salads and no dessert, or no salad and eight desserts.

After we are stuffed, we sing a few songs and then go around the circle telling each other what's going on in our lives. We share our successes as well as problems and challenges and then we spend time praying for one another.

There is nothing greater than having friends who pray for you regularly and think about you often. It isn't unusual to get a phone call or two during the week from a group member asking, "How did it go?" "Did your meeting turn out okay?" "Did you get the deal?" "How was the report from the doctor?" "Did your kid make the team?"

Not too long after we got involved with our small group, one of our members, Betsy, found out she would be operated on for stomach cancer. As she made her preparations, she was told she would need three or four people to take turns staying with her around the clock for several days. She was also told that these friends should be warned that the tasks involved wouldn't be pleasant ones. I knew Betsy was well loved in the church and that she had many friends, so I was surprised when I was one of four she chose to take turns sleeping by her side and caring for her needs. Taking care of Betsy is one of my most treasured experiences. I'm honored to have been chosen.

I hear people complain that they have no friends, that they don't know where to go to make friends. I meet single people who are wondering where to meet a prospective husband or wife. *Well, duh!* To my way of thinking, it's not brain surgery! *Church* is the place to find friends. Friends who are encouragers! Friends who are soul-nourishers. And friends who believe there is Truth and who follow it. Peggy says it best:

> I can't explain everything about what goes on in churches. But I can tell you that the people who go to them are different than the people who don't. I can tell you that the things that happen there can change your life forever, in ways that you don't understand at the time, if you ever understand them at all. I can tell you that if you will let them, the people who are there will lift you up and carry you along and walk beside you.
>
> And I can tell you that if you will come to the house of the Lord, ready and willing to hear his story and to walk among his people, there will be times you will hear his voice.
>
> from *Listening for a God Who Whispers*

I hate to think how different things might be had I never hooked up with my church. Or never belonged to my small group. Or had never met Mr. Tom. Or Helen. Or Betsy. Or Lynn. Or Olivia. Or John and Marty and their girls. Or Pastor Charles. Church is a good place to make friends—even if you have to put up with a few sermons that can only be described in three words: *lo–ooo–ong!*

Keep Your Eye on the Rose

I once read an article in which a young man was describing his mother. He said, "She is the kind of person who doesn't look at the dust on the table, but instead, looks at the rose in the vase."

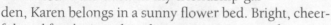

My friend Karen is that kind of person. She immediately sees the flower; she'd never notice the dust. In my friendship garden, Karen belongs in a sunny flower bed. Bright, cheerful, and fun-loving, she tolerates warm summer breezes and demands little upkeep. By nature, she is a nurturer, a motivator, an encourager. She is constantly doing things for others, always accentuating their goodness—making herself vulnerable, so that as a result of her example, they begin to realize their own potential.

For several years, she served as assistant to my Bob when he taught a large Sunday school class. Over time, she became an intimate friend of those one-hundred-plus college kids. She helped them unearth, within themselves, servant hearts that enabled them to serve their Sunday school teacher and his family in an hour of great need. During the weeks of one of Bob's most serious hospitalizations, one of these young people came every night to sit with Bob, sing to him, and walk me to my car. Others ran errands, tended to children, and did the heavy work of moving our entire household from one residence to another. Years later, many of these now thirty-something adults are still making a significant difference in the lives of others—using the gifts that Karen helped them to recognize.

When I think of her, I am thankful that she listened to the lessons taught by the Master Gardener. She has discovered His secrets about seeds and knows that those that He plants within each of us will do their work—even without human intervention. But Karen has allowed God to use her to inspire others, encouraging them to open themselves to the energy of the Creator so that they may become exactly and completely what He intended for each of them.

I pray that I may follow Karen's example—looking for the rose, guarding my eyes from seeing only the dusty dry places, being a model for others, claiming for myself the promise of Philippians 1:6:

"Being confident of this, that he who began a good work in you will carry it on to completion until the day of Christ Jesus."

Anatomy of a Friendship
Written to Peg,
on a significant birthday, from Joy

A trip from Cape May
With milk on my dress,
Arriving New York,
I'd never have guessed
That spending the day
With the president's wife
Would change the forever
Part of my life.

Sick ride on the subway,
A day at the fair,
Talking for hours,
Daring to share
So many life secrets
And those of our friends,
Supposing the tales
Would wane with the end
Of an int'resting day
With some int'resting folk,
But life was to play
A wonderful joke
Ordaining a friendship
Of awesome dimension—
A joyous adventure
Defying convention:

"My Bob" and "your Bob,"
An unlikely pair.
Tearing the curlers
Mid-night from our hair.
Kaboodles of kids
And picnics to make
For Saturday boating
On Old Hickory Lake.

Driving shifts overnight
To Daytona and back.
Sleep break: two adults
With five kids in a stack!
A later trip south
On which Bob was to preach
While his prayer warriors lounged
On a heavenly beach.

Shopping as Lucy
And Ethel for laughs,
Using each other's
Credit for cash!
Girl slumber parties
And late, midnight feasts,
Sharing our bed
With Sue's feline beasts.

Oh, we've traveled, travailed,
We've partied and pryed,
Giggled and gossiped
And laughed 'til we died.
There are worlds I've experienced—
Discoveries, no end—
That I'd never have known
Were you not my friend!
Happy Birthday!

Love, Joy
March 8, 1994

It's a Mother Thing

She was perfect! That's what I thought when I first saw my only daughter, Leigh, right after she was born. A tiny, lovely six-pound bundle of pink humanity! I remember thinking, *There is no way I'll ever be this happy again.* I thought myself a most fortunate mother, and I felt that I could never love her more than I did at that moment. But was I  ever wrong! I have discovered through the years, I love and respect her more with each day that passes.

Don't let me mislead you. We have had our share of differences, especially concerning "important stuff" like clothes, makeup, hairstyles, her choice of friends, and the boys in her life. There have been days so full of laughter and joy that I couldn't begin to express the flood of overwhelming love I had for her in my heart. There have been nights of the soul when our relationship was cold and unfriendly and lonely; we felt hurt and out of touch with each other. I wondered during those times if we would ever really be friends.

But we have become friends, and what a delight she has been in my life. I have watched this lovely person grow and blossom into a fine young woman. She is a wife, a mother, and a homemaker, an artist, a writer, and a pastor to children. Like most mothers I know, she has managed to stretch herself in so many directions, there isn't much time left for herself. Leigh is basically a giver. She knows how to give her heart and her ears to listen to the lives of others.

I must admit the word *listening* has never been tops on my priority list of words. I have always been a talker. Somehow I have had the idea that talking was something you did while you thought about what you should be saying! Bob used to say (teasing me, I think!) that I should learn to knit, so I would have something to think about while I talked. Leigh, on the other hand, is good at listening. By nature, she is shy, quiet, and soft-spoken. She doesn't enjoy publicity or calling attention to herself.

Whether baking cookies with her two young children, or planting a wildflower garden, or sharing a picnic on a warm summer day—she gets to practice her listening skills quite a bit, since it turns out, both of her children are big talkers. She has let me know, in a tactful way, of course, she believes they inherited their need to converse constantly from their maternal grandmother. Britt and Annie talk to big people, little people, elderly people—all people. As Leigh often has said, they force people to be open and friendly! At the end of the day, she tries to save enough energy to hear her husband, as he shares his hopes and dreams for their life together. Occasionally, she still counsels with her four brothers, for whom she has served as "vice-mother" (a name given her by her father during her growing-up years). She offers them emotional support and never, ever betrays their confidences. Finally, she takes time to allow her mother the use of her ear as a sounding board to work through the problems that arise from being alone. In many ways, we have begun the process of role reversal. She is becoming the mother, and I, the daughter. (Growing up is overrated anyway!)

Not too long ago, as she was leaving my house to make the trip back to the farm where she and her family live and I was helping her put the babies in the car, she said to me, with a lilt in her voice, "Mom, I did something this morning that was so much like you, it scared me." We laughed at the idea of that, and as I watched her pull away, I thought about what she'd said. It occurred to me that in a humorous way, she might be saying that she thought she hadn't always met my expectations for her—expectations that might include being like *me*.

If I am totally honest, I must admit, I would be pleased for people to say I was like her! She is, at thirty-six, a long way ahead of what I was at her age. She possesses qualities and strengths and a resiliency that I have worked all my life to own. I hope she knows from my words and actions that she is more than I dreamed possible.

That little girl that was put in my arms all those years ago, the one who used to tug at my apron strings now tugs at my heartstrings. I have come to realize this tug never goes away. It's a mother thing, and I'm tied to her for life!

"Let's hold on to each other ..." (In a note from Sue to Peg as they watched for their children to come home from their wanderings.)

Postcard to Peg

Nantucket: October, 1996

I have discovered that my brain was not dead, only sleeping to escape the chaos around me. And my soul, when watered, straightened right up like a refreshed plant, given water. I may even bloom again. Who knows?

Gloria

The Garden Gate

The garden gate says, "Welcome to my garden!" There must be those openings which invite us to take a detour into the quiet sanctuary where the fragrance of comfortable relationships is the aroma therapy we need to heal our spirits. The garden gate is also a boundary, a protection against predators and pests that would nibble away at the garden of friendship. Enemies like jealousy, neglect, anger, misunderstanding, envy, and stress must be gated out. They must not be allowed to gnaw at the tender shoots of friendship.

When Friendship Fails

It is a death of sorts. Only there is no body. No funeral. No graveside service. And consequently, no closure. Cause of death may be listed as irreconcilable differences, disappointment, misunderstanding, deep hurt or pain, but the reason for the problem is often quite unexplainable.

It happens in gardens too. Certain flowers don't seem as hardy as others; one day they look fine, and the next, they wilt and look as though they've been totally ignored. At first, I try giving them more water. When that doesn't help, I try pinching them back to encourage new growth. I even try extra food to strengthen the root system. But still, they wilt and die, and I never understand exactly what happened.

Likewise, certain relationships don't seem as hardy as others. They lack endurance and strength for the tough places. As with my flowers, I anguish at their wilting, trying to find remedies that will revive them. Could it be the root system? Was our original commitment weak? Did we fail to nourish each other with unconditional acceptance, loyalty, and faith? Were these ever really present?

I know how painful death can be. Bob's death was not easy, but I can bear the pain because it is bathed in the hope that we will be together again someday. But when a friendship dies, I don't know what the outcome will be. It's as though someone I love is missing in action, and I feel the loss deeply.

When I think of Bob, there is joy. When I think of my lost friend, the very remembrance robs me of the joy we shared. Though we are both physically alive, something vital has been taken from us. A sense of failure and emptiness prevails.

It is only slightly comforting to know there are lessons to be learned in such a loss: the need for tolerance and patient understanding; the need to be more aware of the perils of the other's journey; the need to listen, to forgive another's humanity, and to move on past the pain and disappointment of failures and shortcomings — to search for a wisdom that will allow me to see the other person through the eyes of God.

The *bad* news is that we are hopelessly incapable of the grace it takes to be a perfect friend—or even an adequate friend.

The *good* news is found in Romans 8: "In His Son, Jesus, God personally took on the human condition, entered the disordered mess of struggling humanity in order to set it right once and for all. . . . Those who think they can do it on their own end up obsessed with measuring their own moral muscle, but never get around to exercising it in real life. Those who trust God's action in them find that God's Spirit is in them—living and breathing God!" And the *best news of all* is that "this resurrection life we receive from God is not a timid, grave-tending life. It's adventurously expectant, greeting God with a childlike 'What's next, Papa?'" (THE MESSAGE).

Perhaps the next adventure will be a friendship renewed and joy restored!

In the Father's Arms

My Bob is the best hugger I know. As a seasoned co-hugger of the indiscriminate type, I'm a qualified judge. Even our quadriplegic friend, Joni Eareckson Tada, swears there is no hug that "looks nicer or feels better" around her neck than one from Bob. However his hugs are lavishly and selectively bestowed. He only hugs when he really means it.

One of Bob's favorite *hugees* is Peg Benson. Looking back over our long years of acquaintance, I have been trying to remember just how that came to be. I can't point to a moment in time when his genuine affection for her first blossomed, but I remember one night in particular when Bob's arms around Peg spoke what none of us could find words to say.

Peg, my Bob, and I stood huddled together in the hushed hallway of Nashville's Memorial Hospital. An hour earlier, the doctors had confirmed the results of her Bob's biopsy—a malignant melanoma—and at this, Peg's first moment away from her husband's bedside, she could finally break down and wilt into the arms of a friend. We sobbed together as she projected a long list of insurmountable fears for the future of her young family. My Bob held her tightly, and we did our best to comfort her and promise that things like insurance and taxes and changing the storm windows did not merit her concern. She needed to concentrate on making the remaining days count with her husband and five children.

In the Lord's timing, Bob's projected six months stretched to fourteen years, and during that time, we watched as the stubbornness and strength of hope gradually relieved the terror that initially gripped Peg's young heart and transformed it into a mature, confident trust in the wisdom of a sovereign God. God was faithful, and when the time came that He called Bob to Himself, a loving heavenly Father chose to continue to express His care through the occasional warm embrace of a strong pair of arms, which hold her as the Father whispers, "I love you . . ."

Friends make big deals out of little accomplishments! Joy said, "Peggy, you can do anything you make up your mind to do." And she has! She's learned to take care of insurance, taxes, and termites. She can balance her checkbook and make financial decisions. She travels alone, gets herself to unfamiliar cities and hotels, writes, and speaks. She's even learned to use a computer and an answering machine (but she's never going to trust an anytime teller!). She says, "Best of all, I've learned to snorkel. Bob, you would be so proud of me!"

Our Aunt Laura

Laura should have had a dozen children, but life took a different turn than she had imagined. Her skills at homemaking and her love of children are evident in the ways she loves and cares for the people in her life—the same kind of love and care she gives her home and garden.

By nature, Aunt Laura, as she is known to the Benson family, is a nester. Her nesting instincts have been fulfilled in her home, for it is certainly one of the "coolest" nests in town. Her artistic touches are everywhere, and all around are cozy reminders that friends are welcome there. Her mothering instincts are evident too, for even though Laura has no children of her own, she has *many children* who are her nieces and nephews and the children and grandchildren of her friends. A trip to Aunt Laura's house is a real adventure: there are pencils and paper, scissors, coloring books, glue sticks, office supplies, art paper, and crayons. Collections of dolls at rest, on various small chairs; old hats and purses, odds and ends of jewelry, and many other treasures are ready to capture a child's imagination. There are fruit juice and cookies, good books and music, and a ton of love and attention. When you leave her home, you leave knowing you have one ally, one believer, one dreamer, one person in your corner. She doesn't give up on you and she lets you know it.

I'm not sure of the exact definition of an aunt, but I do know the definition of an "Aunt Laura"—a really with-it, warm, southern lady who makes sure you know that you are valued, you are wanted, you are important—you have a friend!

(Come to think of it, I really should amend my opening statement. Our Aunt Laura does have children . . . dozens of them!)

Thank You

September 2, 1986

Dear Joy, Mac, Shana, and Kristen,

How lovely to put a bookmark in the frenzy of our lives—to spend these hours with you all and other dear friends who have been the constant of friendship over the days of our past. We have watched these children from baths in the kitchen sink and driving Matchbox cars down the beach through the days of kites and two-wheelers, into curling irons, lipstick, whiskers, and hormones. We've packed diapers, booties, knickers, dolls, puppets, electronic games, ballet slippers, guitar strings, diaries, plaster of paris, contact solution, retainers, and neckties. Now, we seldom have to pack for them at all. We've gone from worrying about broken necks to broken hearts. We've traded baby-sitters and parents' night out for car keys and blind trust.

This time our circle had a new first—one of us missing; a widow stood alone, representing a family circle grown and flown. Through this, as through all the stages, the fibers of friendship have proven to be strong enough to hold us like a cable holds a mountain climber who sometimes has to throw his whole weight against it when the footing is less than sure.

I used to think it belittling that notes like this one to say thanks were called bread-and-butter notes. But this morning it seems somehow appropriate that thanks for such a gift as yourselves should be synonymous with the basics of life. Truly, you all and your friendship is like *the staff of life* and *the something elegantly extra* that makes the quality of our days rich and full. You are dear ones.

Thank you,
Bill, Gloria, Amy, Benjy, Suzanne

Gloria

To Celebrate Again

Holidays are still hard for me! Christmas without Bob is almost unthinkable. He had definite ideas about how he wanted his family to center in on the Christ of Christmas. If there was one thing he knew how to do, it was to make a moment. He did know how to celebrate!

Peggy

As the holidays began to roll around that first Christmas without him, the signs of Christmas only saddened me. But gradually, I began to welcome them again. The hustle and bustle reminded me that somewhere there was light and warmth. And peace. Laughter and joy. And hope. While it was difficult to find the energy to buy a tree and decorate the house, it was still relatively easy to shop. (I suppose it will be time to call the undertaker when I lose interest in shopping.) The thought of thirteen of the world's most adorable grandchildren unwrapping their treasures gave me the needed incentive!

However, I couldn't quite handle the thought of getting out the treasured manger scene that Bob loved so much, and soon the rumor got around the family that I was dragging my feet about the whole idea of Christmas—perhaps not even going to put up a tree. For my children, that was going just a little too far, and they decided to take matters into their own hands.

One afternoon they all showed up. About twenty people arrived unexpectedly on my doorstep! Tom brought the tree in his pickup and hauled it through the basement door and up the steps into the living room, where he placed it in the center of the room. In a matter of minutes, the family paraded through the house with tree trimmings, lights, supper, kids, enthusiasm, and NOISE! Someone even had the good sense to dig out my favorite Andy Williams Christmas tape, the one Bob and I had used to start the festivities for twenty years.

The grandchildren insisted I sit in a decorated seat of honor and enjoy a scrumptious tray of goodies while the magic took place. Right before my eyes, the living room began to take on a feeling of festivity.

The next year, as the holidays approached, the kids asked, "When do you want us to decorate for you?" I replied, "Maybe I can be tough enough to get it done by myself." By this time I was working at a little florist-gift shop and had begun to eye and buy a few new ornaments. Finally, I would have decorations that matched!

This meant saying good-bye to all the old things my children had made through the years. *It might be fun to give the little darlings their ornaments back for their own trees*, I thought as I laid them aside.

Tom helped me buy a tree and get it to the living room. After he left, I popped a chicken pie into the oven and made a nice fresh fruit salad. While supper was baking, I put on ole Andy, and to the tune of "Happy Holidays," began to gather and sort my lights and ornaments—all the while praying that I could hold on to the spirit of hope I was beginning to feel in my soul.

The phone rang, and I recognized a sweet, soft, tearful voice.

"Peggy?" It was my dear college-age friend, Amy Gaither. "What are you doing?"

"I'm trying very hard to be a big girl and decorate my first Christmas tree without Bob and the children. What are you up to?"

Her voice quivered a little. "I just called home and my family is decorating our tree today, and it's the first time in my life I haven't been home to help. It makes me so sad and so homesick, I guess I just needed to tell someone."

"Amy," I said, "what is your opinion of chicken pot pie and Andy Williams?"

Amy came over and we ate in the dining room on fine china, with crystal goblets bathed in candlelight. We had such fun decorating my tree at our own pace. We talked about our lives and all the good and bad times our families had shared through the years. At day's end, we sat for awhile in the glow of the fire and the twinkling lights. Then I hugged her good-bye. She thanked me for filling the empty places in her heart, and I thanked her for helping me light the darkness in my soul and for reminding me once again of the Source of our light.

The third year, I looked at myself in the mirror and said, "Okay, Mrs. Benson. Quit whining. Grow up. Get a grip. Snap out of it!"

I made my trek to the grocery—Kroger, where all us swinging singles shop!

I bought my chicken pot pie—Marie Callender, of course!

Went over on Charlotte Avenue—where prices are the best.

I bought my tree. Brought it home. Put it in the stubborn tree stand. Brought it up the steps (in a sheet so that the walls wouldn't be scratched—a trick I learned from Bob Benson). *All by myself!* It was time to bring out my new, everything-matches, not-a-handmade-one-in-the-bunch ornaments. I lit the fire, started the music—Vivaldi's *Gloria* this time! (Sorry, Andy!) I baked my chicken pie, made a salad, set a place in the dining room with china, crystal, and candlelight.

I began to feel an unexpected, calm reassurance deep inside—a feeling of comfort and peace. At last, a feeling of being at home with myself. A voice I have come to recognize and know and trust spoke to me, saying, "I am your light in the darkest of times and if you will let Me, I will teach you . . .

> *to celebrate the season,*
> *to celebrate the moments,*
> *to celebrate the fact that you are not alone,*
> *for I will be with you always*
> *and I will be your everything*
> *—one day at a time!"*

The Trellis

Usually the most creative, free-growing friendships are also the most profuse bloomers. Unstructured and adventuresome, these free-form growers most need the support of a place to entwine; they need the structure of a trellis of dependability but the freedom to feel their way along. If allowed to thrive, they will eventually create a lovely shelter from the heat and wind.

A Perfect Vacation

Fellowship Group retreat
Colorado, May 1991

Time . . . precious time
. . . time to write . . . and read,
. . . time to set new goals and personal
*   expectations,*
. . . time to nourish friendship.

Ah . . . friendship!
. . . friendship that smothers and then
stands back to give breathing room,
. . . friendship that risks laughing at any
*   silly thing at all,*
even our own foibles.

Sue

We'll remember . . .
our voices repeating, "Can you believe this place?"
shopping for T-shirts
puzzles
breakfast in the jacuzzi
talking theology, leadership, consultantship,
Sue's book, Joy's project, and Evelyn's patient.
puzzles
strawberries 'n cream 'n brown sugar
smiling for pictures by the creek
Shana and friends
mindless chatter
serious discussion
puzzles.
A perfect vacation.

She Kept Her Promise

Peggy

When my husband, Bob, was so ill during the last three months of his life, we spent most of the time checking in and out of St. Thomas Hospital. The last trip from home to the hospital was in process when out of the blue, in walked my good friend Barbara. She just *happened* to be going by—unless you believe God sends His dear children along! The emergency crew was frantically working on Bob and I was pacing the floor praying they would get him stable enough to make the move to the hospital.

"I'm staying until they get him ready; then I'll take you to the hospital and stay with you until you get a report from the doctor," Barbara announced.

Several hours later when Bob saw us, he said, with a weak little grin, "Boy, am I glad to see you two. I was so scared!"

Surprised by his remark, I said, "Honey, I didn't know you were afraid to die."

Bob thought a minute, and said, "I'm not afraid to die; I'm afraid to hurt!" Then he turned to Barbara and said, "Promise me something. Will you take care of Peggy and stay close to help her through all the things she will have to face alone?"

Barbara never hesitated. "I promise you I will, Bob." She has never gone back on that promise.

Describing Barbara is a challenge. She is perpetual motion. Like Maria in *The Sound Of Music*, she is like a wave on the sand or a moonbeam in the hand. She defies description.

There is both mystery and magic to our friendship and our time together. Any given day together is like scattering a package of wildflower seeds on the ground and waiting anxiously to see what they might turn out to be. It's a surprise package. A real deal!

When my son Patrick was about four years old, I asked him what his Bible verse was. "Do good and share what you got!" he replied. (Is that what it says in Hebrews 13:16?) Though I'm not sure about Patrick's version, I *am* sure that Barbara lives out that verse to the hilt.

She's shared her life with me in so many ways over the last ten years. Most mornings, we share a walk and a muffin. Sometimes it's a salad at lunch or maybe a piece of pie in the afternoon. If her husband, Tom, is away we might share a prime rib dinner, or if it's Tuesday, maybe a brown bag special from the Sonic. We enjoy each other's gardens and divide our plants with one another. We often spend time together with our children and grandchildren, telling the same jokes and stories over and over because we believe some things bear repeating!

As good friends, we can share our inner selves, be as shallow and silly as two school chums or as serious as any two adults who trust each other with their deepest secrets. If you promise you will keep it to yourself, I'll let you in on *our* deepest secret: We've taken a vow to put on our swimsuits and go to the beach together as often as we can, for as long as we can get there, wrinkled thighs and all! And when we can't go anymore, we are going to check into the same old folks home because we believe we can have fun anywhere—even if we can't remember *why* we're having fun.

A promise kept, lives shared, grief eased. My life would have been a lot more dreary and dark all these days alone, without Barbara. She has cared, consoled, calmed, cried, comforted, cajoled, and cheered me. Long before there was an organization called Promise Keepers, there was Barbara. A friend who keeps her promise!

A best friend doesn't wait for a call for help!

Count on Me

I may not have the answers
to the questions you will face.
I may not be the one to drive away your fear.
My list of imperfections is too long to erase.
But, you have my word, I will be here.

Lord, I know sometimes it seems
there's not much I can do.
I'm not a hero or a name.
But I'm a house upon a rock
when I rely on You,
a constant friend
whose promise will not change.

Count on me
in this world of shifting sand.
Count on me
when you need a steady hand.
I will work and pray,
mean what I say,
and live unselfishly.
Right the wrong.
Standing strong;
You can count on me.

Suzanne Gaither Jennings

A friend is one to whom we may pour out the contents of our hearts, chaff and grain together, knowing the gentlest of hands will sift it ... keep what is worth keeping and with the breath of kindness, throw the rest away.—Patsy Winfrey, The Nashville Tennessean

Pruning the Garden

In most relationships, as in most gardens, pruning is needed from time to time. Confronting—cutting away the suckers and out-of-control tendrils that choke and drain a friendship of its vitality—is not a simple or easy task. The gardener must use great skill so as not to cut the taproot or the sap-conducting main stem and thus destroy the plant. But when problems can be taken care of early by a loving and careful hand, the plant becomes stronger for the pruning and produces more blossoms and heartier, more delectable fruit.

Ebb and Flow

Change! You can count on it! Life boasts very few things that are absolutely dependable, but change is one of them, and it is the one we seem to fear most.

Joy

The moon and the ocean both provide exquisite models of the rhythm of life—consistent in their waxing and waning, advance and retreat, ebb and flow. But in our brief earth journey, most of us just haven't quite been able to get the hang of it. We dread the ebbing, fearing the flow will never return. We want it to be all flow. Especially in our relationships, we demand a constancy that is impossible.

The life of the spirit, says Saint Exupery, . . . is intermittent and only the life of the mind is constant. . . . The spirit . . . alternates between total vision and absolute blindness. Here is a man, for example, who loves his farm, but there are moments when he sees in it only . . . hard days of work. Here is a man who loves his wife—but there are moments when he sees in love nothing but burdens, hindrances, constraints.

We light upon a situation, an occupation, a relationship that is to our liking, and we want to cast that first kiss in stone. Somehow, we are able to subscribe to the myth that the honeymoon can last forever. We demand permanency as a security against loss when, in reality, the only way to keep what we have is to allow it freedom to change and grow.

By the time a child reaches the age of twelve, she has likely experienced the disappointment of a treasured relationship gone awry. Often it is the result of having clutched too tightly what she loved so.

Friendship is perhaps the most vulnerable of our cherished relationships. Unlike the unions of marriage and family, its only ties are of the heart. And the stronger our need for a friend, the more tenacious our grip. But close observation of lasting friendships reveals people who are able to allow others to come and go in and out of the days of their lives with ease and grace. No grand entrances or notable exits; they simply pick up where they left off!

Friendship is not a machine—you can't just add more memory, more megabytes to make it better. Boxed in, mechanized, it cannot flourish. It has personality that must be given the freedom to flourish—like a garden, it must have space to grow and change.

If the joy is in the flow—the moments of great advance, the rush—then the maturing and growing is in the retreat, the pulling back, the ebb, during which there is a grand preparation and anticipation of the next exciting surge forward. Just as the mighty ocean wave retreats to empower its next forward motion, it is not folly to expect the sun to arrive tomorrow—following the darkness, without which our joy at the light would be diminished!

In God's infinite understanding of the human condition, He reaches out to assuage the dread and fear of change: "Trust me," He says. "I will never leave thee nor forsake thee." " Come to me . . . and I will give you rest." "In my presence is fullness of joy."

In His lovingkindness, He does not deliver us from the bleak and barren of a winter experience to immediately sear us with the intense heat of summer. Rather, He demonstrates to us the ingenuity of the divine plan. In the natural world, we call that part of the plan spring or fall. In our hearts, we call it the presence of God.

> *Thou wilt shew me the path of life: in thy presence is fulness of joy; at thy right hand there are pleasures for evermore.* Psalm 16:11 KJV

Even the garden needs a rest—a time when seeds sleep briefly and safely in assorted envelopes, and bulbs snuggle in the paper nests of the potting shed. Sometimes friendships need a winter's retreat—resting places from the persistent demands of one another's cares and burdens.

Learning to Like "Alone"

Peggy

I married Bob Benson when I was seventeen. I went straight from my mama to Bob, and a year later we had a little Bob. Being alone and lonely was something I had never experienced. With five children, our home was full of noise, energy, and other people's kids! In those days, it was almost impossible to have five minutes alone in the bathroom, much less quiet, reflective time *alone* to collect my thoughts, process information, and nourish my soul.

After thirty-five years of togetherness, it was a tremendous shock to realize that home had become a place of quiet and solitude. I felt as though I had received a long jail sentence. As time passed, I realized it might be all right to finally have a chance to read and write and actually think a whole thought through to the end, without the interruption of telephone, oven timer, or a little person with a must-be-answered-right-this-minute question. Maybe I could adjust to this business of learning to be alone.

To my surprise, God chose an able and loving woman to help me adjust—my sister! Bo (whose real name I'll never reveal!) is a very well-adjusted single woman. She never found anyone to "float her boat."

Bo was only four years old when I married, more like my child than my sister. By the time she was five, I had my first baby, so she loved to hang out and play dolls. Every summer, from the time Robert was born, she spent a portion of her summer at our house, quickly becoming part of our everyday life. The work time, the play time, the car pool time, the homework time, the prayer time, the garden time, the vacation time. Whatever the Benson family was doing, she was doing it too, because she was part of us.

As I began the process of adjusting to single living, my sister taught me that it takes a certain strength to motivate yourself and that "learning to believe in you" is not always as easy as it might seem. This is especially true if you have had a husband like mine, who constantly told me how much he loved me. A girl can get addicted to that stuff very quickly! Okay, I admit it. I was spoiled!

When my cheerleader moved to heaven, it sometimes seemed impossible to get out, much less motivate myself to move on with my life. Bo helped me realize there were steps I could take to becoming a whole person—steps apart from marriage, children, social achievements, or economics. These are the things she taught me, not from a list in a book, but by the way I could see her living out her life.

First, it isn't necessary in life to own a house, but it is necessary to make a home. Even if you rent only one room, it can be your nest and reflect who you are. It should be a place that contributes to a feeling of solace and comfort deep inside yourself. Bo taught me to create space for myself and get to know who I am, apart from being Bob Benson's wife or a Benson kid's mom. With her encouragement, I learned to make my own celebrations, moments, and rituals—to understand that being a whole person on my own was reason enough to celebrate.

It's been over ten years since I set out on the road to discover myself. Bo has been there for me every step of the way. Together, we've raised my kids, cleaned my house, weeded my garden, and painted my old piano. We've taken vacations, watched old movies, eaten lots of popcorn (buttered and unbuttered), read books and discussed them, laughed until we cried, and cried until we laughed. We've decorated for Christmas, undecorated after Christmas, buried our mother and more recently our dad.

Together we picked up the pieces after Bob's funeral, that lovely spring day in March and, as I look back over these years, I realize that a large part of my wellness is a result of drawing on her example and her strength. She has allowed me this privilege because we share a bond that goes beyond the fact that we have the same parents. It's a bond born out of my respect and admiration for a person who made up her mind long ago to grab onto life—as a *whole* person, not as an extension of someone else—and live it to the fullest.

The saints were rarely married women!—Grandmother Benson, age 95

Sharing Cuttings, Seeds, and Plants

Seasonal gardeners love to share their plants as old friends love to share meaningful relationships.

"Oh, I wish you could know my friend, Joan," is akin to the veteran gardener saying, "When I divide my iris, I want you to have a start of this incredible, blue-bearded hybrid."

When you treasure something—a rare flower or a wonderful friend—you simply want to share the joy with someone else. Many of our friends come into our lives because they were friends of a friend.

I Would Give My Child
the Gift of Friendship

I would give my children the gift of friendship. I would have them know the joy of sharing their hearts without having to speak words, to know they're forgiven without having to ask forgiveness, to know they are valued without having to achieve.

I would have them know the assurance of a clasped hand, the meaning of an exchanged glance, the stirring of a shared joy, the empathy of an unexpressed disappointment.

Gloria

I want them to grow up surrounded by the honest exchange of ideas and opinions, the risking of new experiences and adventures, the delight in enjoying the simple things, a circle of familiar friends. This will help them know that friendships are necessary, possible, and worth the struggle that all great relationships demand.

I would have my children experience and enjoy friendships that cross age, race, gender, cultural, and religious lines—friendships that grow because they're nurtured, thrive because they're valued, and survive because they're resilient. I would like our circle of friends to be the kind that would help our children prepare the soil of their hearts for the seeds of friendship and help them learn to care for the tender sprouts of friendships in their young lives.

I would like our home to be a place where friendships can grow, blossom, and mature—a garden of friendship where strong-rooted, deep, old friendships thrive alongside new, experimental ones, hardy ones with fragile ones that need a lot of care.

I would teach our children that the greatest Friend of all is the God of the Universe, who cared so much about relationships that He chose to walk the dusty roads of earth with us. He confined His great mind to our finite thoughts and expressed His unfathomable truths in the words of a human language. He exchanged the grandeur of heaven for a simple carpenter's home, a friend's guest room, and a borrowed tomb. And He traded having us all as His slaves and servants for enjoying us as His friends.

Most important of all, I would have my children know the great joy of an honest and intimate relationship with the Friend who sticks closer than a brother or sister.

In the garden of friendship, stained knees, dirt beneath the nails, unsightly messes—the unpretty—are welcomed. We are on amiable terms with heat and cold and mud and dust. No need to be concerned with looks or outward appearances among friends. This is the potting shed where problems are solved and life is nourished, rearranged, rejuvenated.

White Silver Bells

Lilies of the valley remind me of my mother's friend, Mrs. Overly. I called her "O." O had the biggest patch of lily of the valley in the world (at least I thought so when I was five), and she let me pick—to my heart's content—tiny bouquets of perfect little ivory bells! I loved to wave them under my nose and sniff their exquisite fragrance. While I picked and sniffed I sang my song.

Sue

> *White silver bells*
> *Upon a slender stalk*
> *Lilies of the valley*
> *Line my garden walk*
> *Oh, don't you wish*
> *That you could hear them ring?*
> *That will happen only*
> *When the fairies sing.*

Now I have lilies of the valley of my own, growing under my magnolia tree. These particular flowers belonged to my mother-in-law. They used to line the front walk of her home in Mt. Vernon, Indiana. Even before that, they graced her yards in Plymouth and Whiting and Silver Lake. Mom dug up those flowers and replanted them every time they moved!

Even though I'm not an honest-to-goodness gardener, I must admit that because of my love for the flower and the pull of tradition—perhaps fifty years of it—I did manage, one day years ago, to dig up a few clumps, wrap them in newspaper, transport them to Nashville, and plant them.

Each year when they bloom, I pick tiny bouquets, wave them under my nose, and sniff them for all they're worth. When I'm all alone, I sing my song, certain I hear the ringing of tiny bells.

All the Men I Love
Are Married to My Best Friends

Peggy

Now that I am single again, I get a lot of questions about a possible man in my life. Frankly, I'm not sure I have enough time left to whip one into shape! I have tried to imagine the kind of person I could marry. I suppose it is natural to think of Bob and the qualities he possessed—some good and some not so good. (Maybe there is no such thing as a *bad quality*. That may be an oxymoron.) It's amazing how many of Bob's positive attributes shine strongest in the memory, while all the things that irritated me have grown dimmer and dimmer! At my age, I've had ample time to reflect on my own marriage and those of close friends. From Bob, I've learned that I would want a mate or a boyfriend whose qualities include patience, perspective, and a positive outlook as well as charisma, confidence, and a colorful character. All the better if he were retired and ready to walk on the beach or travel Europe. I would like it if he didn't ask me where I was going every time I went out the door. He would know me well enough to know I would be back later, and I'd tell him where I'd been and what I was doing and who said what. He would soon learn I would tell him more than he wanted to hear!

And what have I learned from others, especially husbands of close friends?

Wayne Buchanan makes me laugh out loud. That's good for the soul, you know. Very scriptural! He refuses to let me get bogged down in the whiny widow syndrome. Wayne lets me be ridiculous and a bit of a tease. He likes me just the way I am!

Tom Pate allows me to pop in and pop out of his and Barbara's life. He encourages me to say what I am feeling, even if it isn't always positive. I never feel judged by him. Somehow he seems to know when I need to let off steam. He's probably the kindest person I have known. Bob used to say about him that Tom was better by nature than most of us are by grace. I'm glad we are friends.

My husband had a best friend who was like a younger brother to him. Buddy Vaughan has become my brother and confidant too. He has made himself available to me when I have needed to yell out my frustrations, or I have felt angry or hurt, disappointed or left out. He listens when I grumble and complain. Then he teases me until I get over it. He has helped me see it's time to move on!

No list of men in my life could possibly be complete without Bill Gaither. Bill helps me remember the most important part of life—the good times! He is a storehouse of information and remembers all the wonderful moments our families have shared. He is the person who, more than anyone, has helped to preserve the memory of Bob. He feels deeply for me and lets me know it. With him, I never feel unwanted, unneeded, or out of place. Once he said to a group of mutual friends, as he watched Bob MacKenzie walk me to my front door, "Poor little thing. We've got to find her somebody so she won't be lonesome." I hope he knows he *has* found me somebody—himself!

Bill, Wayne and Buddy, Bob and Tom have been Jesus to me. I am humbled by their love and concern for me and my children. I finally feel like a whole person again.

Finally, there's Bob MacKenzie. Bob was my husband's dear friend and dreaming buddy. They were the driving force behind the creativity of the Benson Company for almost fifteen years. They logged many a mile on the buses of various music groups, spending hours talking philosophy or details of business deals. MacKenzie has now become my dear friend and confidant. He is a sort of *other husband* to me, and I am the *other woman* in his life. Thanks to Joy, I am allowed this place in his life! I can say most anything to him, and often do. He doesn't always agree, that's certain, but he does always listen. He definitely has an opinion, and usually, I want to hear it (though I don't always do what he says). No wonder my Bob loved him so; he makes me believe I can do most anything if I put my whole heart and soul into it! He pushes me beyond myself and sees in me more than I see in myself. When I am with him, I feel special and even pretty at times—a feeling that is hard to come by when you're a widow. I always come away feeling like a girl, and when you're my age, it's good to feel like a girl again!

An ideal mate—let's face it—is a tricky assignment, but if I were looking for a new man in my life, these are qualities I would hope to find:

Bill Gaither's love of the moment;
Buddy Vaughan's spirit of fun;
the humility and kindness of Tom Pate;
Bob MacKenzie's ability to see a person through eyes of love;
and of course, as you might imagine (having been married to a very funny, clever man) my ideal man must have the wit and humor of Wayne Buchanan. He is a little crazy, but I like that in a person! Besides, he is married to Sue, so he gets to be crazy a lot!

Gloria says Peggy is looking for Mr. Right. Peggy says make that Mr. Price is Right. Sue says she thinks Mr. Close will do.

Rugged Lady

She was tall, fine, beautiful—and rugged. When but a girl, she sewed together a muslin cover, lashed it to the wire bone-work over a wagon and started across the country to homestead in Wyoming with her husband and two small babies. Years later I was to sit at her knee and listen to her tales of wolves, coyotes, heat, and Indians; of nights when lonely cowboys would join the family for meals around the campfire and spin yarns about their cattle drives.

Gloria

There was not much sentiment or softness about her. Hers had been a difficult life in an untamed country, and there was no time or place for frills. She was a master of all the arts of survival. She could create the latest fashion from a feed sack, make lye soap from hog fat, turn a hovel into a home. She could dress a wound or bring down a fever. Once she bound a severed finger back into place, and by prayer and the sheer force of her will, made it grow back where it belonged. She hated dishonesty, weeds, and dirt. In her household there was never a floor left unscrubbed, a hole left unpatched, or a wrong left unpunished. There was never a job that was too hard for her or a demand on her that her energy couldn't match. She nursed a bleeding ulcer for sixty of her eighty-some years. The only way we knew of it was the empty Maalox bottles we sometimes saw in the trash.

The summer before she died she decided to put a new ceiling in her bedroom. Rather than ask her children who lived twenty miles away for help, she ordered heavy-duty plasterboard from the lumberyard, sawed it into manageable squares, climbed a ladder, and nailed them into place. She stripped the cracks, painted the finished ceiling, and told us about it later.

I admired her and stood in awe of her, but I never felt she liked me very much. Now looking back I know that I misunderstood so much about her. As a child at special times such as Christmas and birthdays, I'd try so hard to find the gift that would finally win her approval. But no matter how hard I'd try, the response was always the same. She'd unwrap the gift, look at it, return it carefully to its box, and put it away. She never wore or used the things I gave. She did seem to enjoy getting money, so my parents often gave that.

She had special places where no one was allowed to look. We didn't go near her purse. Certain cupboards and closets were full of locked boxes and were irrevocably declared "off-limits" to prying eyes and inquisitive hands. It was only after she was gone—and even then out of legal necessity—that we intruded with fear and trembling upon the privacy of her holy of holies. What we expected to find I'll never know, but there in their original envelopes were all the gifts of money we had ever given her. Sorted, totaled and bound by rubber bands, the bundles were labeled, "This is to bury me"; "This is for the house payment"; "This is for the fuel bill." And piled neatly in their original boxes, like hoarded jewels in a priceless collection, were all the gifts we had ever given her. Going through the stack was like leafing back through the years, with the corresponding memories sifting out between the pages.

She had loved us all along. It was just that the crucible of the times in which she'd lived had forged a coat of armor around her. And the same shield that had protected us all from danger and hurts had also kept her from breaking out to tell us what she'd felt in her heart.

That last week, she'd mowed her lawn, weeded her garden, and taken a butcher knife and uprooted the dandelions in her yard so they wouldn't go to seed and spread the next spring. On Sunday she put a roast on to cook and went to church. When the service was over she fixed dinner for Grandpa, washed the dishes, straightened the kitchen, took off her apron, folded it neatly on the foot of the daybed, and lay down to rest. She died as she had lived—her soul and her house in order and her work done.

Now that I have lived a half century myself, I see the seeds of her were well planted in me. I find myself unable to leave until the work is done. I feel guilty throwing things away that could be repaired. I do things for myself instead of asking for help. I tolerate pain and hate to complain. I love the truth and detest dishonesty.

There are seeds of her that I have tried to keep weeded out of my life. I want to say things that matter to the people I love. I try to relish and use every gift I'm given and to have few places in my house or my heart that are off-limits to my children or grandchildren.

I hope, however, I am a true pioneer. I want to be the best storyteller my grandchildren ever knew. I would wish to be a survivor who doesn't flinch at the sight of blood or cave in at a time of crisis. In many ways I have become her. And, I hope, in many ways I have taken advantage of the trail she blazed to be all things she would have been had she had the chance—most of all, I would dare to love and express my love.

Grandmother's Wisdom

Peggy

My mother-in-law will be ninety-five this summer. With an eye for color and beauty, she is a wonderful gardener. And in these last quiet days of her life, though legally blind, the garden has become a special friend. She is still in the garden most days that weather permits. It offers peace and comfort and a sense of belonging. Recently, I spent a rainy day with her when we sat and talked about gardening. These are some of the wise words she spoke that day. I have a sense of urgency when it comes to remembering her words. I write them down, for myself, for my children, and maybe for you:

Surely no man-made garden is more lovely than a hillside of wild poppies—but if a man, or better yet a woman, makes a garden, it is more selective, more personal. It is hers and God's and once she gets her hands in the dirt, she is in league with God and with life.

I believe I'm too domestic to be soulful. Pop used to think I'd rather clean and dig in the garden than to "invite my soul" [i.e. spend time in quiet meditation]. He may be right, but I think I can do both at the same time. Gardening relieves us of petty anxieties—from worries, hurts, and disappointments, and for a short time, at least, we see the world from a whole new vantage point—and there is a feeling of unaccountable peace.

I am one of those people who can do little work when snow is falling. It's as if I have to supervise the whole job!

Machines and I are not compatible. We regard each other with great hostility.

I've turned over so many new leaves, I'm resting on a whole bed of them!

Gardening gets harder as I get older! I have begun to get arthritis in my knees and finally went to the doctor. He looked at my x-rays and said, "Well, Mrs. Benson, I see you have a little arthritis!" You could have fooled me. A great amount of it is what I thought I was having! Did I just leave a participle dangling? Oh, well, Winston Churchill did it all the time.

Maintenance Tips for a Friendship Garden

You may have to do things you don't want to do. Sue often begins one of her favorite stories by saying, "If I could tell you the times I have put myself out for these three women!" (pause) "Just kidding! However, I do remember a time they, and our husbands, did something for me they didn't want to do. I have to admit I stooped to using my illness and the fact I might die of cancer to get what I wanted. My last wish, so to speak, was to attend a Willie Nelson concert, and even though my friends hated the idea, they cooperated and ended up having a wonderful time. Fortunately, I didn't die. They've never forgiven me for that!"

To Be a Good Friend . . .
- Smile often; laugh aloud now and then; giggle, even.
- Become aware of several things that you especially enjoy. Watch for others who enjoy those same things.
- Identify an acquaintance who has a need you can supply. Offer yourself. (Hint: Start with the obvious—your sister, spouse, neighbor . . .)
- Learn to enjoy being alone with yourself. Identify what elements of living enrich your life. Incorporate them in your daily routines. If you are happy being with you, it's likely others will enjoy your company too!
- Forget what you give and remember what you receive.
- Be the one who is there doing when others are saying, "Is there anything I can do?"
- Listen—even in the silence.

Peg recently declared that if she had tried to create the perfect formula for friendship, she'd have missed it by a mile. "No, make that at least 300 miles!" she quipped. "When I met Gloria, she lived 300 miles away, already had a reputation as a brilliant songwriter, was gorgeous, and had it all together as the perfect wife, mother, and professional. (Later, I learned I could scratch the word *perfect!*) I stood awed, offstage, never suspecting our lives would become so entwined.

"Joy and I just happened to 'fall in love' with each other on what was supposed to be a polite business date, arranged by our husbands. I was pregnant and nauseous, and Joy arrived soiled and smelly, having spilled an entire glass of milk down the front of her dress. Who would have thought ...?

"I first saw Sue, elegantly posed at the top of a winding staircase. She was having a conversation with three men who stood admiringly at the bottom of the stairs—or stares! Immediately, I liked her brash, clever wit, but it was intimidating. I knew I could never match it. I was right!

"It is shocking to realize that, had I set out to cultivate the perfect group of friends, I would likely have omitted most of the people who have become my dearest companions. Fortunately, in God's sovereign plan, friendships rise naturally— often out of what we see as unnatural alliances or circumstances. What a relief to know that He is the one in charge."

Formula for friendship: Relax! Be yourself! Rejoice in His choices!

Autumn's Quiet

...Friendship Savored

Relaxing from the Work of Friendship

No season brings more joy to the gardener than the harvest. The backbreaking work of cultivating, fertilizing, weeding, mulching, and watering has paid off, and the plants are at their outrageously colorful best. The circus of autumn plays itself out for all to enjoy in that "window of time" between the heat of mid August and the first frosts of October. These are the days to gather bouquets to enjoy now and to dry against the gray days of winter. It is time to save and label seeds for another spring, for we have come to trust the process of the seasons. Although there is a melancholy urgency that tells us we must not put off taking time to celebrate and absorb the garden, we also have seen proof that gardens—and friendships—will thrive in another season if given half a chance.

Friendship

It's to my friend that I may speak my mind,
Knowing that she will not revel in the flaws
she sees there.
I need never be afraid
To bare my soul before her,
But she would not for morbid entertainment
Uplift the cover and intrude the sanctity
of my heart.
I know my friend is always there
(A comforting thought),
But the depth of our friendship is not measured
In numbered rendezvous.

Our hearts are close—
A nearness that transcends proximity of human form,
For thoughts, like mountain nymphs,
Dance from the dewdrops in the meadows of my mind
To those of hers. Those meadows
Need not run to meet each other,
And yet they are all one:
The meadows, the dewdrops, and the nymphs.

My friend can bear to watch
As burning tears burst from my eyes;
She does not fear to fix my compass
When I have veered off course,
Or to remind me
It's not a broken compass,
But that I have forgotten
That North is North.
Yet she does not live to say to me, "You're wrong!"
We are as two great painters, working in the same room.
We share at times our paints
So that each may achieve a perfect color,
But we are creating separate masterpieces.

Gloria

To My Mother's Friend

Dear Frona:

Congratulations on your ninetieth birthday! How I'd like to be there to help you celebrate. I've been thinking a lot about friendship these days—thinking about writing a book on the subject with three of my friends. According to those who supposedly *know* these things, true unconditional friendship is rare, and most people go a lifetime without it. It occurred to me as I scribbled my thoughts, that my own patterns for friendship were established as I watched my parents love and nourish those around them, and be loved and nourished in return. I believe God orchestrated something wonderful those many years ago when He brought you and Harry into our lives.

When I speak of you, I say "my mother's dear friend," and yet you are my dear friend too. Some of my favorite recipes are in your handwriting. Some in Mother's writing are assigned to you. A special one that will undoubtedly be passed from generation to generation is your custard. I deliver it to friends and acquaintances when the situation seems hopeless—when I have no idea what to say—*because Mother said,* "Custard will go down past the lump in your throat." Each time I make it, I think of you. I think of her.

So thank you for recipes . . . for an elegant wedding shower . . . for my first experience with spoon bread . . . for wonderful smelling beds when I came to spend the night . . . for picnics in the backyard . . . for "putting up with" . . . for prayers . . . and for being Mama's good friend. For tangibles and intangibles alike, thank you. Thank you for showing me Jesus and for planting so many wonderful memories that have lasted a lifetime.

Love you,
Sue

Frona's Baked Custard

Beat slightly to mix:
    3 eggs
    1/2 cup sugar
    1/4 tsp. salt

Scald (crinkly film forms on top):
    2 cups milk

Stir together and add:
    1/2 tsp. vanilla, if desired

Pour into 1 1/2 qt. baking dish, and set dish in pan of hot water (1" deep). Sprinkle a little nutmeg on top. Bake at 400° for 30 to 40 minutes until inserted silver knife comes out clean. Soft center will set as it stands. (I often double the recipe!)

Go forth into the busy world and love it. Interest yourself in its life, mingle kindly with its joys and sorrows. Try what you can do for others rather than what you can make them do for you, and you will know what it is to have friends.—Ralph Waldo Emerson

A Comfortable Place

The occasion was a farewell for friends graduating from seminary. We realized we would never see each other again in quite this setting—all together in one place.

We were young, full of hopes and dreams, setting out to conquer the world.

"Won't it be great to be in heaven someday where we won't have to say good-bye?" someone conjectured.

"Wonder what it will be like!" another answered.

Immediately there were all manner of speculations flying through the air: "Certainly streets of gold!" "No more three-room flats!" "You can all come to visit me in my mansion." "You won't be able to miss me in my long, flowing robes and opalescent wings!" "Who knows, I may be so inadequate in life that I have a tacky, gaudy crown!"

Oh brother, this is getting out of hand, I thought to myself. *It's bordering on boring.*

"Well," I quipped, "mansions, gold streets, and angel wings aren't my thing. I'd settle for a nice bustline!" The room grew silent.

Then Bob replied quietly without the least hesitation, "Well, that would be heaven to me!" We all burst into laughter.

It occurs to me, as I think back on that occasion, that friendship is a very comfortable place in which you can afford to express your most private thoughts aloud.

Friendship is the inexpressible comfort of feeling safe with a person, having neither to weigh thoughts nor measure words.—George Eliot

One If by Land, Two If by Sea

Mark Twain once said, "Everyone should have at least two friends—one who sees eye to eye about everything—another who disagrees about nearly everything." I have always thought a lovelier notion is that everyone should have a friend whom one can trust with both responses—comfortably!

Joy

For me, that person is my sister, Marge. Though we shared a bedroom when we were children, we were eight years apart in age and became best friends after we had both married and joined the same profession. Common genes is probably one of the lesser contributing factors to our friendship. Of course, we both catch ourselves being our mother. And our husbands lodge a list of common gripes that have something to do with a "take charge" gene that intimidates all the other in-laws and outlaws. What they don't understand is that it is just two "servant hearts" at work, getting the job done more efficiently and effectively than if we lay back and waited for all the more relaxed sorts to do it.

Marge and I do have much in common in that we both lead frantic lives, are overcommitted and underendowed with time and energy to complete the constant flow of tasks we take upon ourselves. We are readers, writers, talkers, and eaters (she cooks; I'd rather clean toilets). We are both ardent lovers of words and champions of young people. But our strongest addiction is also our strongest connection—maybe it *is* somehow genetic: our souls wither and die if at least once every six months or so, we cannot stand on a rocky coast or a sandy beach and drink in the restorative, healing powers of an ocean. ("You lead me beside roaring, undulating waters; you restore my soul. . . .")

We know that some people in the world neither share nor understand our need. They are more attracted to mountains or deserts or quiet woodland streams or bustling cities—places we agree make lovely vacation spots—but when one needs nourishment for the spirit, there is no place like a rocky shoal, standing in mockery against the pounding surf, or a silent, underwater reef, teeming with colorful sea life. It was during one of our many seaside retreats together—a warmish, windy October day on a West Coast shore—that our rock-solid perennial friendship was tested to the limit.

We were perched in a sea grass nest on a sand dune, high above the Pacific, lying on our backs in our windbreakers, trying to see which of us could most accurately guess the whodunit of the Agatha Cristie mysteries each was reading.

Suddenly, one of us sat upright and suggested, "Let's do a word thing. If you were to identify the one word in the English language that best characterizes me, what word would you choose?"

That sounded like fun, so we agreed we would cogitate awhile, then share our choices for each other. We read most of the afternoon away in our idyllic perch, stopping now and then to recall some past moment of amusement or joy, or rail briefly about something of insignificance that worried us like a wart.

At last, the moment had come to share our words, and we wrote our choices in the flyleaves of our books—just to keep ourselves honest. I, being the most anticipatory, begged her to go first. Her choice shocked me.

"Thorough," she said matter-of-factly.

"Thorough? You're kidding! *Thorough???*" I screamed against the wind.

I couldn't deny that it was a very accurate fit for a part of who I was, but was that the best she could do for the whole of me? This? From my beloved sister—my very best friend in the world? Such a disappointing response. And of the myriad of possibilities—words like brilliant, clever, ebullient, gracious, lovely, alive—she comes up with *thorough!* I wanted to roll her off the cliff. She giggled at the intensity of my distress.

"Well, let's hear what gem you've chosen for me!" she teased.

In my burst of comic rage, I had forgotten. I checked my flyleaf . . .

"You," I announced, "are tolerant!"

And of course, I was immediately proven right, since her reaction was much more moderate than mine, though she disliked my choice as *thoroughly* as I had hers! We laid back in rollicking laughter until our ears were wet with tears and our hair was full of sand.

Maybe Mark Twain was right—maybe one of each kind of friend is a better idea!

How fortunate we are when we love somebody who loves us back!

The Other Woman

My husband had several loves in his lifetime. Before we were married he had a reputation for always having girl-friends in several Christian colleges across the country. Of course, that was before I moved in for "the kill" and quickly put a halt to that sort of thing.

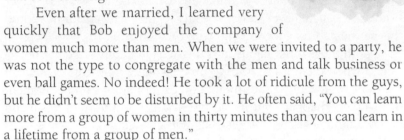

Even after we married, I learned very quickly that Bob enjoyed the company of women much more than men. When we were invited to a party, he was not the type to congregate with the men and talk business or even ball games. No indeed! He took a lot of ridicule from the guys, but he didn't seem to be disturbed by it. He often said, "You can learn more from a group of women in thirty minutes than you can learn in a lifetime from a group of men."

One of his favorite women was Gloria Gaither. These two were kindred spirits. They spent hours talking philosophy, ideas, issues, and reading material, not to mention really important stuff like hopes and dreams and where we might go on our next vacation. Frankly, Bill Gaither and I got a little bored by their deep conversations. We did everything we could to distract them, get them to refocus, and put the attention where it belonged. On us! Alas, it was to no avail, for when they got rolling on ideas it was a long, exciting process.

Only two months before Bob died, we were on vacation together talking about an important dream that Gloria and Bob shared. Their dream had always been to publish books together ... books that might make a difference in people's everyday lives. Now that Bob has finished his journey, Gloria dreams double for both of them. And she is helping me acknowledge and share my dreams. She is one of those people who not only takes time to tend her own dream, but gives encouragement, confidence, and inspiration to oth-ers as they share their dreams with her.

My friendship with Gloria is different from my other Nashville relationships in several ways. Ours could be termed a long-distance friendship, given the fact that it is a long distance from Nashville,

Tennessee, to Alexandria, Indiana. It's a long way to go for a cup of coffee and sparkling conversation, but I have found it well worth the journey and go as often as I can.

We share the same feelings about a lot of things. We both feel deeply and passionately about our children. We just may be two of the last "earth mothers" around, since everywhere we go, we collect a pack of children like butterflies on a butterfly bush.

Our relationship is strong enough to endure either great intervals of silence or almost constant togetherness. At times, I have realized it has been too long since we've had a visit, and yet we can pick up a conversation almost in midsentence, as though we have never been apart. There never seem to be any reentry barriers for us. Could this be the nature of a good and true relationship?

Both the Gaither family and the Benson family are quite determined when it comes to finding time to make moments. We share the same philosophy about them: you cannot always find a moment or make one happen, but if you put yourself in the right place and do your homework, *a moment is more likely to find you!*

During the last weeks of Bob's life and all through the week of his homegoing celebration, Gloria was there giving me courage and comfort, and as spring gave way to summer, she insisted I join her family on vacation. Our families had vacationed together for years; this time, however, there were no children and no Bob to share it. Besides, this was no ordinary vacation; they were going to Nantucket Island, one of Bob's and my favorite places! It was a place so familiar to me that I could see Bob around every corner, walking along the beach or standing at the end of the pier in the foggy morning light.

That trip taught me to *be with my grief*, to quit running from it, to stop hiding. While I was learning, it was important to be with people who would allow me to pour out my heart and express my pain and disappointment. Gloria understood that, when it comes to dealing with the grief process, the human soul doesn't fare well in the fast lane. It takes time, tears, energy, and determination to allow grief to do its work in our lives.

Gloria believes in me and dreams for me. She prays for me even when I have no strength to pray for myself. I couldn't help thinking of myself as half a person when Bob died. She saw me as whole, with my own unique possibilities. Or weirdness! She said, by her actions and words, "You have value; you are not just an extension of Bob." She gave me the courage to think of myself as strong and resilient. She made me dare to risk again, and I will always be grateful to her . . .

for standing by and holding me up
for pushes and pulls and prayers
for thumps on the head and smiles and hugs
and finally having the courage to say . . .
enough is enough . . . there's work for you to do!

> *Be strong and courageous and get to work. Don't be discouraged by the size of the task. For the Lord our God is with you, he will see to it that everything is finished correctly. 2 Chronicles 20:15–17 (TLB)*

A Letter to My Daughter

From the moment I first held you in my arms, still drenched in birth, until now as I watch you drive away to the appointments you've made with life, mothering you has been my life's most awesome, fearsome, and joyful adventure. I didn't know that first day what mothering would mean, though I was eager to begin. You seemed so fragile then, so small and trusting—depending on me for every life-sustaining need. I thought at first you'd break.

"Be sure to support the little head," they told me. But I was soon to learn that you were tougher than you looked and could out-squeal, out-sleep, and out-endure me, ten to one. In fact, those first three months, I wondered if I'd ever finish a meal or a night's sleep again.

The teaching began immediately. I had studied to be a teacher, but it seemed to me that there was never a classroom student as hungry to learn as you. Before you could speak, your eyes asked the questions and your tiny hands reached to touch and learn, taste and see. It wasn't long, though, until your cooing turned inquisitive, every babbled sentence ending with a question mark. Your first words were: "What's that? What's that?" Soon your questing vocabulary grew, and you were begging, "Teach me something, Mommy. Teach me something."

I would stop to teach you: numbers and names of things—textures, shapes, sizes, foods, furniture, pets, trees, flowers, stars, and clouds. Soon you were teaching me. Teaching me that when the lesson stopped, learning kept on going.

You taught me to see the miracles I'd stumbled over every day. You taught me trust and delight and ecstasy. You held a mirror up before my attitudes and role-played all my reactions. You taught me what it meant to live what I verbalized, to believe what I preached, to internalize what I lectured.

You, who came to me all wet from birth, baptized the common things with natal freshness and with the shower of your laughter, washed away the barnacles of grown-up cynicism and the dust of dull routine. You made things new. You gave me an excuse to be myself again, to skip down forest trails or sled the frozen hillsides, clean with snow, to splash through springtime puddles—barefoot-glad—and guess at where the shooting stars must go.

You gave me eyes to see the realness of people once again, to look beyond their faces' thin façades. You saw the child inside the aged, the longing and the passion entrapped by gnarled joints and failing eyesight. You recognized profundity and wisdom in the giggly, teenage baby-sitter, beauty in the plain, and creativity in the timid. You showed me that the generation gap is an artificial invention of our culture and bigotry a perversion of nature's celebration of variety.

I have helped you learn to crawl, toddle, walk, run, swim, dance, ride bikes, and drive the car. I have encouraged you to stand tall, walk alone, run from evil, dance for joy, ride out the hard times, and drive yourself on when you felt tempted to give up. I have been there waiting when you crossed the road, climbed off the school bus, came in from dates, and returned home from college. Now, about all I can do for you is to *be there*, because gradually you have come to be your own person—not so much my child as my friend.

A Love Lost

How utterly irreplaceable is a true friend! Bob Benson and I were kindred spirits—especially at the dinner table. We ate together often, and we liked the same kinds of foods. Peg and my Bob are adventuresome eaters—the gourmand variety—but Bob Benson and I, meat-and-potatoes people, always stuck together at banquets and parties.

Joy

He was president of my fan club—a position left yet unfilled. He used to touch my chin lightly, shake his head, and say, "What a face!" I never asked him exactly what he meant; I preferred to believe it was a compliment, since it was always accompanied by a smile and a tone of genuine affection.

Sometimes the bonds of friendship include irrevocable loss—which heightens our awareness of how precious such affection is and reminds us of the richness of human connections, one of God's great gifts.

Collector's Items

My mother-in-law, who is ninety-five, expresses herself beautifully. Some of the things she has said through the years are priceless. She is not only a clever and witty woman but a woman of wisdom and insight. Her intuitive bits of philosophy I shall treasure always. To make sure they aren't forgotten, I have written them down so that my children and grandchildren will have a record of them.

One afternoon I stopped in to visit with her.

"What have you been doing lately?" she inquired.

"Well, I've been cleaning closets," I said. "Honestly, I don't know where I get all the clutter. I keep shoving it back into the corners of the shelves. Bob and I did a major discarding and selling off when we moved from the house on the lake, and then again, seven years later, when we moved from our house in Brentwood to the condo in Jefferson Square. Now here I am, going through that process once more! I keep asking myself why I am keeping so much stuff. Where did all these little collections come from? I manage to get rid of excess furniture—let's just say my children rid me of excess furniture; but it's all the little collections of things that I've had over the years that seem to be overwhelming me now. I look at them and wonder why I ever thought they were so important, and yet somehow I have a hard time letting them go."

Mother loves to philosophize. As she settled back into her chair, I could almost see her sifting through her ninety years of experience.

"Some people profess smugly that they never collect things. They would like to believe they have more self-control than to let themselves get attached to the trappings of life." She paused. "But I would argue the point with them, for every one of us is really a collector at heart."

Mother's eyes narrowed as she continued to ponder the point.

"We humans are real pack rats," she said. "We deny that we are collectors, yet we hold on to the past for dear life."

She paused again, leaned forward in her chair, and raised a finger as she added a final postscript: "We're not limited just to fine china and snapshots or old leather-bound books. All our lives, we are making collections that are far more significant." I drew close to catch her whispered words. " . . . fears, phobias, and suspicions . . . hopes, dreams, and illusions . . . attributes, persuasions, and prejudices."

Since that day, I have recalled many times Mother's ruminations. As a result of our conversation, I have begun to realize something very important: Just as houses must be cleaned and scrubbed and rearranged on occasion, so must our lives be swept and reordered and refurbished. In the process of tidying up, laying aside, and letting go, I am learning more and more to discard the clutter, the jumble, the redundancies of my life and to hold on for dear life to the *life* of my life. And I'm growing in my ability to tell the difference!

It is the simple, basic pleasures of our daily lives, memories and moments with those we hold dear, that are the significant, valuable treasures. I've decided I would be willing to give up nearly every collection I have, except one—my family and friends. I guard these relationships intensely. I work earnestly to keep them nourished, and I value them greatly. They are truly a collection worth keeping.

My husband used to say, "In this life if you have two or three good friends, consider yourself fortunate." I am indeed blessed! My friends are part of that *life* of my life that gives me warmth, color, and texture, courage, comfort, and strength, joy, tears, and very often, laughter. Laughter in large doses! If I were asked what I cherish most, my answer would surely be my faith in God, but without so much as a comma between, I would have to add my exquisite treasure of friends and family. This is a collection I intend to keep!

I Can Hardly Wait for Christmas!
(one of Sue's famous, crazy Christmas letters)

We're sure there are those who remain friends with Sue just to receive her yearly Christmas letter. Unlike the usual ones that brag about the new house, the kid that made the team, the pro- 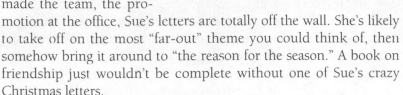 motion at the office, Sue's letters are totally off the wall. She's likely to take off on the most "far-out" theme you could think of, then somehow bring it around to "the reason for the season." A book on friendship just wouldn't be complete without one of Sue's crazy Christmas letters.

Happy Holiday Greetings, Family and Friends!

It's here! The Christmas season is here! Our house is dec-orated and we're ready. No one enjoys it more than we do. I can't wait for the church concert where we'll see and hear our friends perform. I can't wait for Carlana's traditional Italian dinner and breakfast at the Opryland Hotel with Bill and Gloria . . . and Kate and Dick's open house . . . and the party at Judy's . . . and unwrapping gifts with Joe and Alice. I can't wait for the Nashville Symphony concert with Ronn Huff, Amy Grant, and Vince Gill (pant, pant!), and I can't wait to wear the new sho-ort black vel-vet swing dress with the hot pink satin collar and cuffs.

Christmas, as you may know, is not without worry. This may seem like a small thing to you, but my biggest concern for the past couple of Christmases is that Wayne would find out that I didn't actually bake the Christmas goodies myself. I thought myself fortunate when I found this dumplin' of a woman who loves to bake and has come up with a surefire mar-keting plan. She makes the rounds of the offices, hones in on those of us with stacks of work on our desks and *fingernails out to there*, and she knows immediately we'll pay big bucks for her services. She waddles in unannounced, a knowing smile on her lips, and with the flair of a QVC hostess, presents us with a list of cookies and candies that are the exact recipes we ourselves used to make when we had the time. There are places to check off what we want: pecan tarts, chocolate chips with nuts, chocolate chips without nuts, Russian tea cakes, and on and on.

It works out well for me because Wayne goes off on a business trip for a day or two and when he comes back, the pantry is full. I add a few convincing touches, such as stacking mixing bowls and measuring cups in the sink, dusting my eyebrows with flour, and dabbing a touch of vanilla behind my ears. Yes, it's slightly dishonest, but you do what you have to do, if you know what I mean.

Well! This year I was the one to go off on a trip, and when I got home, Wayne proudly led me to the pantry. There, lo and behold, were stacks of labeled boxes: pecan tarts, chocolate chips with nuts, chocolate chips without nuts, Russian tea cakes, prune bars (wait! . . . prune bars?); and . . . well, you get the picture. There was neither flour on Wayne's eyebrows, nor the aroma of vanilla wafting from behind his ears. So the question is, did he spend the weekend baking and cooking, or does he too have a relationship with dumplin' lady? And one more thing! I don't recall seeing prune bars on dumplin' lady's list (however, my reaction to that is "good thinkin', Wayne!"), so I may never know the truth. There are some things in a marriage you leave well enough alone.

Can't wait for Dana and Barry to arrive, and for Mindy, and Jon, Becky, Cara, and Kirby to "move in" for a few days. Can't wait for the gift giving! But think of it: the greatest, most expensive gift we have ever received, or will ever receive, is the gift of Jesus who gave us salvation and the assurance of eternal life!

Love,
Sue

Peggy and Sue believe they are gifted. Sue says she has the gift of criticism; Peggy has the gift of exaggeration.

Maintenance Tips for a Friendship Garden

When a serious problem comes up, examine the friendship and decide if it's worth fixing. Once in awhile it's not; it's irreparable, given the circumstances. Usually giving it a bit of cooling down time helps gain perspective. Sue tells about trouble in a very important relationship: "My dearest friend from childhood and I had a disagreement of I'll-never-speak-to-you-again proportions. Because it was philosophical in nature, I worried that it was hopeless. I was sure I could bring her to my viewpoint. She told me to back off. After a cooling-off period, a greeting card came from her, and it just so happened I had one addressed and ready to send to her. Next there was a tenuous phone call. Then another. At last I found I would be in her city on business, and when I called to say I was coming, she asked, 'Do you have some extra time? Can you stay with me?' I did and I could. We talked late into the night and spent till noon the next morning in the wing chairs by the fire, coffee in hand, picking up where we left off. Repairing the relationship was worth it and then some!"

Speaking of friends is often a delicate matter. Sue has often teased, "If you can't say something nice about a person, come sit by me." Of course, as she says, she would "walk on her lips" before she would repeat what anyone told her. The rest of us, on the other hand, sometimes have difficulty recognizing that fine line between harmless information and gossip.

Friends are never won and rarely kept by our speaking ill of them. Sometimes we do it on the spur of the moment and without malicious intent. Later, we are surprised, embarrassed, even appalled at the injury it has caused. Taking turns

at being president in good and permanent standing of the Foot-in-Mouth Club, all four of us have often felt the remorseful sting of having hurt someone we cared about. I guess that's why the watchwords of Scripture are so hard on the tongue!

Obedience to the wisdom of James chapter 3 should be our motivation. Sinners that we are, we should better have clothespins clipped to our tongues or our mouths sewn shut. Perish the thought!

"There is no such thing as an 'all-occasion' or 'one-size-fits-all' friend," says Joy. Each of my friends has unique qualities that enrich my life in very different ways. My business/writing partner, Imogene, and I used to make an annual Christmas shopping pilgrimage to Atlanta. On the four-hour trip, we could nearly complete the outline for a new book. As we planned, I drove and she wrote. We'd spend two days shopping, two nights working on the book, and arrive home the third day with half a rough manuscript together and our Christmas packages ready to put under the tree. We made great fun out of being an "efficiency machine"!

Evelyn doesn't do books, and we've never shopped together, but we're great partners for skiing and snorkeling. She's a stronger swimmer, and I'm a better skier, but we're a team. We've worked out a rhythm for enjoying long hours together on either a reef or a mountain. Peggy and I have fun shopping, but we're dawdlers and don't get much accomplished. She finally has the hang of snorkeling—likes it better if there's a float nearby—but she flatly refuses to take up skiing.

If I want someone to talk to late at night, I call Evelyn. Peg is kind about being routed out at midnight, but the next day, remembers nothing you said. Imogene is an early-to-

bed, early-to-rise person. Of course, if I want the hot news, I call Sue, who is happy to accommodate at any hour!

Listing the special qualities of each friendship is a fascinating and gratifying thing to do. It's like counting your blessings!

Cut some slack! Sue has always done unpredictable things without thinking. Right out of the blue, she does some crazy, unplanned stunt that is bound to embarrass those around her. Once Wayne and Sue were having dinner with friends in a restaurant in Denver when Sue recognized voices wafting from a table that was a level below theirs and on the other side of a curtain. Without thinking, she hiked up her skirt, stuck her leg through the curtain, and plunked her high-heeled shoe smack in the middle of the table. It grew very quiet until a voice said, "I only know of one person in the world this could be. Sue Buchanan!" The couple dining with Sue and Wayne were embarrassed beyond words (as was Wayne) and could have chosen never to speak to Sue again, but being true friends, they have come to relish the story and retell it with great flourish at every opportunity.

Winter's Promise

... Friends in Peril and Pleasure

Friendship in the Hard Times ...

Gardens are still gardens under the snow, and a friend is still a friend when there are no parties going on. In fact, it is during the severest weather, when the ground seems frozen and it looks as if spring will never come again, that the trees are deepening their roots and the plants and shrubs are gathering nourishment to support another season of growth. Just as the winter does not kill the orchard, neither does death, separation, divorce, or failure kill friendship, but forces it to deepen and become better rooted in the soil of God's love. Seeds that have fallen are being prepared to lose their hard casings and sprout. The resting time when friendship and plants lie dormant for a season encourages them both to put out new shoot, come spring.

A friend loveth at all times. Proverbs 17:17 KJV

There Are Moments

There are moments in friendship
I want to save
like snowflakes
in the cup of my palm,
hoping they won't melt,
knowing they will . . .

Joy

It's Not Easy Being Friends

It's Friday afternoon. It's been a hard week at school, and I'm dragging my weary body from the car to the house. The telephone is ringing. Already! I think I haven't the strength to lift the receiver, let alone deal with another human being. I let the machine answer.

"Hey, Bob and Joy! It's Linda. How about joining the Raymers for a fast sandwich and a movie? Something! Whatever! We haven't seen you guys in forever. Say six or seven-ish? You choose the place. Let us know!" *Click*.

This was their third attempt at connecting with us in as many hectic weeks. I called Bob. We dumped an immutable plan to spend our first free evening in a month at home, comatose on the couch, and met the Raymers at a restaurant. We ate. We talked. Ate and talked. And talked some more. We never got to the movie. We came home—much later than we intended. Revitalized. Content.

Three long days after Christmas, 1987, sixteen members of the MacKenzie clan, grandparents to toddlers, have enjoyed more family *togetherness* than even the holiday spirit can endure.

I lock myself in the bathroom to clean the facilities and gain a few moments of solitude. Emphasis on *few*. Shana knocks on the door.

"Mom, Sue wants to talk to you." She hands me the phone.

"Joy, just wanted to let you know I've made lunch reservations at Miss Daisy's Tea Room. Girls only. Leave those nasty men and babies. Dana, Mindy, and I will be expecting you!"

Overwhelmed with Sue's generosity—and the prospect of escape—I stammer something dumb like, "Sue, this is too much. I can't let you . . ."

She interrupts.

"If you're not there at eleven forty-five sharp, I'll never speak to you again!"

She hangs up. We are all there—at eleven forty-four!

The house is crawling with musicians. Bob is working on a huge recording project with a group from England. I am running a hotel, restaurant, and laundry—nothing out of the ordinary for either of us. The normal, wall-to-wall teenage activity and upper decibel levels of stereo play are wearing my frayed nerves.

Suddenly the door opens. Unannounced, in stalks John Coates, his arms loaded with bags of food and pots and pans.

"Papa John's Taco Catering Company at your service, ma'am. Clear the kitchen counter and turn on the oven!" A chorus of cheers goes up from the teenage contingent. Hurrah for their favorite meal.

My favorite cook gets a huge hug. And a few happy tears.

Bob has had croup for a week. Evelyn, mother of five, grand-mother of millions, and caretaker of invalid patients, shows up with a jug of her delicious, to-die-for veggie soup.

We come home from a missions trip to find that Wayne Buchanan has replaced our scraggly, frostbitten bushes with a row of robust hollies.

Our daughter, Kristen, is getting married. My friend, Shirley, dismantles her own bridal veil to create the perfect one for Kris, makes alterations on the dresses, irons, answers phones, cleans, serves food, waits on family and guests—makes herself the ultimate servant to our entire family for several days.

Friendship, especially in books, is usually addressed in terms such as *kindness, tenderness, sympathy,* and *affection.* Life experience and friends who are remarkable models of the concept cause me to believe that it might, more precisely, be associated with *perseverance, self-sacrifice, expense,* and *exhaustion.*

Gather up the gifts your friends have to offer—laughter, touching, listening, crying, good conversation, good casseroles, celebration, and put them in a big basket (figuratively speaking, of course). Use them as you need them, but for heaven's sake, don't expect everyone's gift to be the same!

The Warning

A note found by Bob and Joy upon their return from a missions trip to Eastern Europe, summer of 1987.

"Go into the world and preach," He said.
"To every creature, break the bread."
We've prayed for you as the lambs you've fed,
But it's watching the slides that we all dread!

We said, "Lord, send them. They'll do just fine."
(Some must stay home and trim the vine.)
Yes, the burdens of the world, you've alleviated.
We just hope your stories are abbreviated!

We added mulch. Your plants we wetted.
We planted shrubs. The cat we petted.
We used your pool—we are indebted,
But we won't watch your video 'til it's edited!

Sue and Wayne

Helping a Friend
Through Tough Times

Hugger-mugger looks and sounds like a made-up word, but it's not. It's an honest-to-goodness, in-the-dictionary word that means "confusion; muddle; disordered; jumbled"—in other words, one of life's *tough times.* The dictionary doesn't say so, but my personal definition of the word is, "I'm so confused I don't know from one minute to the next whether I'll be hugged or mugged."

Hugger-mugger is a great word for positive thinkers because positive thinkers hate to use negative words—words such as cancer . . . divorce . . . bankruptcy . . . addiction. Even the word *problem* is difficult for some people to say. I work with one large company that has made a rule that problems will be referred to as "opportunities." *Hello, Mrs. Buchanan, we've had the opportunity to lose another order and mess up your account for six months in a row.*

My friends are up to their elbows in hugger-muggers much of the time. I only know one person whose life seems to be perfect. She's healthy. She has money to burn, and I've actually hidden in the bushes outside her perfect home hoping to hear the crash of pots and pans hitting the walls, or at best, the sound of nagging voices. No such luck. Just melodic whistling to the sound track of *It's a Wonderful Life.*

It seems at first glance there must be hundreds—perhaps thousands—of hugger-muggers; but surprisingly, you can narrow them down to three basic categories: relationships, health, and finances. My friend Joy will argue that there are only two. She says, "If money can fix it, it isn't a problem."

My most earthshaking hugger-mugger so far has been breast cancer. I had a mastectomy, a bad prognosis, aggressive chemotherapy, and reconstructive surgery. Ten months into my treatment, when I was poking through the doctor's desk because I was bored, I discovered his notes, saying he didn't expect me to live long enough to have reconstructive surgery. That was fifteen years ago!

Since that experience, I've become a world authority on helping friends through tough times. My expertise doesn't stem from being such a wonderful, do-unto-others person, but from being able to observe the best possible examples. My friends! They taught me four things:

1. *Do something!* A friend of mine got a call from her boss who had been in the hospital for a couple of weeks. "Bring your notebook when you come today," he ordered. When she arrived he began to dictate a list of names. She assumed these were people to whom he would be sending thank-you notes. Instead, he was listing the people he hadn't heard from.

"They've hurt my feelings, and I want to make sure I ignore them when *they* get sick!" he explained.

Of course, most people don't keep such a list. But it's a startling reminder of the importance of reaching out to others in need. Who doesn't like it when friends send a card, a note, or even a lavish, wildly expensive gift!

Once when close friends were going through a financial setback, my husband and I, after much deliberation as to what we could possibly do to cheer them up, delivered a large box of beans to their front door and hid in the bushes to see their reaction. Times have improved for our friends but when we get together we always laugh about the bean episode.

2. *Be yourself.* Do what *you* do best. In my own situation, I discovered each friend brought a different, but unique, perspective to my hugger-mugger. Each brought a gift. Some were tangible, some intangible; all were a part of my recovery process.

My friend Joy brought celebration. Each time I finished my cycle of chemotherapy, Joy would figure out some new way to celebrate: a nonsense book with a funny bookmark, an animal cracker picnic on my office floor, or a slumber party.

Joe, my neighbor, doesn't do bookmarks and animal crackers. He would think some of Joy's shenanigans downright silly. But Joe knows how to cry, and there were times I needed to cry. Joe would come to my hospital room, take both of my hands in his rough handyman hands, and cry with me.

Some of my friends gave me the gift of casserole. Now I hope this next bit of information doesn't get back to Joy, but Joy's casseroles aren't that great. Kate, on the other hand, is the great Italian mama. Kate was solely responsible for making the lasagna that brought my appetite back to life after chemotherapy. What a gift!

3. *Participate*. My friends not only brought casseroles and animal crackers but stayed to eat them with me.

Sixteen years ago, Bob MacKenzie had a heart attack and open heart surgery. We still talk about the "great summer of Bob's heart attack." While I wouldn't wish that particular hugger-mugger on my worst enemy, that summer gave us some wonderful memories. My husband and I and our group of friends set up our offices by Bob's pool, shared his healthy-choice salads, and swore that if Bob had to give up meringue-up-to-heaven coconut cream pie, *we* would give up meringue-up-to-heaven coconut cream pie. Of course, we didn't keep our promises about the pie, but I guess you could say we did *participate* in Bob's hugger-mugger.

4. *Know when to back off*. Sometimes life's hugger-muggers are irreversible. A child dies. Divorce papers are signed. A business goes down the tubes. Sometimes an illness goes on, seemingly forever.

There are times in life when lasagna won't get past the lump in your throat and when silly books and animals crackers aren't appropriate.

Once when we were going through a particularly tough time with our daughter, a friend wrote a prayer note. It said, "Dear God: Please hold Wayne and Sue close . . ." I still have the note and I've used the idea myself a few times.

When our friend Bob Benson was near death, Wayne and I knew that Bob's family was large and supportive and that the one thing he didn't need was more visitors. We wanted to do *something*. We felt so helpless. Finally we decided to go to the hospital and simply stay close by. Although we hadn't planned to do so, we ended up in the chapel praying for Bob and Peggy, and we sent a note up to the room telling them we were there. Praying made us feel as though we were doing something, which in fact we were.

Prayer is the very best way I can think of to help a friend through a tough time. It costs nothing and it works. Even secular research is discovering that prayer works. But of course, we knew it all along.

Aunt Lillie

One of the best friends I ever had was Aunt Lillie. She wasn't really my aunt, but Bill's. She was actually his great-aunt, his grandfather's brother's wife. Somehow though, she was everybody's Aunt Lillie and our children's best friend.

Never mind that she was an octogenarian and they were just children. The years didn't separate them. They stopped by her house often after school for lemonade, insisted we pick her up in the old convertible whenever we went for ice cream, and together they watched the tomatoes they'd planted grow ripe, in huge pots on her front porch steps. Later, they took their boyfriends and girlfriends for her inspection and approval. When there were too many days between visits, she didn't waste time scolding them because they hadn't come. Instead she would joke about her voice not working because she'd forgotten to use it that day. She said she finally bought a parakeet to talk to so her voice would have something to do.

She had a great sense of humor and a mischievous sparkle in her eyes. Her stories were captivating and she loved making fun of politicians and movie stars who, in her opinion, hadn't a clue what life was all about. She never missed church; she always paid her tithe and her taxes—early! She was always game for an outing to anywhere or a conversation on any subject.

When Aunt Lillie died at ninety-four, the family asked if I would talk about her at our celebration service of her life.

What she had taught us all about friendship was so profound and pervasive that it was like a huge, ever-blooming rosebush that covers not only the lattice but the whole roof of the house. To this large gathering of best friends, these are the words I spoke in celebration of Aunt Lillie.

We come here today to pay tribute to a life that was its own tribute. There is little we can say to fix up or add to the way a person has lived out 34,969 days. Someone has said that what age does to us is just to make us more. If we're selfish, it makes us more selfish; if we're gracious, it makes us more gracious. If we're generous, kind, meek, long-suffering—age makes us more so. If we're short-tempered, cantankerous, ungrateful grumblers, age just intensifies what we already are. Kind, gentle, thoughtful young people generally grow to be kind, gentle, thoughtful old people. Angry, belligerent, grudge-holding young people usually turn out to be angry, belligerent, grudge-holding old people. Age only makes us more so!

So what qualities were intensified by 34,969 days of choices, attitudes, activities, and dreams of this life we come to celebrate?

First, in spite of the longevity of her days, it was hard to think of Aunt Lillie as old. She was joyful, childlike, mischievous, and optimistic.

She thought young, always ready to go someplace, tell a joke, play a trick on us, or start a new project. She was always hopeful—whether it was about the new preacher who'd just come to town, the tomato plants at her back door, or the future of the many nieces and nephews who raided her refrigerator for fresh lemonade. No matter how bad things seemed, Aunt Lillie was sure they would get better. Only such an optimist would, at ninety-two, buy a lifetime membership to Sea World or gladly accept the gold-painted skateboard the retirees fellowship gave her when she moved to Point Loma.

She was a giver. No matter how little she had, there was never a week she didn't have her tithe envelope ready; never a family birthday when her kids didn't receive a fresh, new two-dollar bill; never a reunion or family dinner when she didn't scrape together the ingredients for banana pudding salad and the energy to fix it. When she left for California she gave me a little brown sack. In it was a gift wrapped in tissue paper. "Give this to Benjy on his graduation day," she said. I did what she asked. Inside, Benjy found Aunt Lillie's traditional little plaster figurine of a boy graduate in cap and gown which sits, even now, on the shelf in his room. She always paid her missionary dues at the start of the quarter. She paid her bills before they were due and her respects when anyone in town passed away. It seemed to be important to her to live with everything paid up.

Aunt Lillie kept her mind growing. She never missed the news, nature shows on TV, or reading the paper. She read *Reader's Digest*,

Arizona Highways, The Herald of Holiness, and each quarter's missionary book. She read great books, too, like *The Robe*, biographies, and the Bible.

She taught us what it means to be faithful—faithful to her God, faithful to her friends, faithful to her kids, faithful to her one man, Joe. When we'd tease her about finding her a man, she'd say, "I had my man." Even though she outlived him by longer than most people's life spans, you somehow had the feeling it was still and always would be "me and Joe."

She wasn't a complainer—not about loneliness, not about pain, not about circumstance. Rather, she saved her energy for rejoicing over and enjoying the good things that came along. She took things in stride, whether it was working at Aladdin, where she wove wicks for oil lamps, or losing a precious son to war, or outliving most of her friends. She concentrated instead on the next Gaither or Allen reunion, a bus trip with the retirees group, or going to San Diego to be with son Paul. She remembered the past, but lived in the present, always planning and anticipating the future.

She knew how to delight in simple things: a ride at sundown in the convertible, a chocolate malt from Dortee's, fresh white peaches or caramel corn in the fall, a walk with Paul down on Point Loma, the marigolds and dusty miller growing on her porch step, a piece of raspberry cake at a birthday party. She loved to have the kids stop by with their new girlfriends or boyfriends, wives, husbands, or new babies, and she loved good news!

We are all fortunate to have known her. Most of us here have been her kids. She has preached today's sermon already with her life. She has reminded us that we come from a long line of good people who were true to their word, faithful to their mates, and committed to their Lord. We come from a long line of strong, sturdy folks who loved to laugh, were always eager to help, and who gave us the solid foundation of knowing that through thick and thin, they were there for us to lean on.

Now it's our turn, for "to whom much is given, much is required," and we have been given much. In a world dominated by pushing and shoving, insisting on one's own way, string-pulling and small-time bickering—in a society that is missing the big picture, nickel-and-diming itself to death over things that won't exist tomorrow, I'm thankful to have had models like Aunt Lillie. I'm thankful for those who kept it simple, lived with gratitude, refused to give up, always looked for and found the best in every person and situation, and who lived the old adage: "If you can't say somethin' nice, don't say nothin' at all!"

She told us, "I probably won't be back till they bring me home in a box," and she was right. But this fine box holds a rare treasure: a well-worn, nearly used up antique container that has served for almost a century to house a warm, loving, mischievous, sparkling, generous spirit.

Aunt Lillie was fond of "riddin' out," she called it, and today we will carry to the cemetery, what to her great delight, she started "riddin' out" last Sunday.

She's had her ticket for a long, long time, tucked in the pocket of her soul, bought and paid for by her Father. Her seat was guaranteed, and having it brought her hope during the hard times of her life. It let her laugh through trials, smile at disappointments, and celebrate with great joy the small victories of her days. But Sunday, like a little kid at Disney Land, she pulled out her ticket, climbed aboard a chariot, and, with no fear of flying, took the trip she's been planning all her life.

Today, as the few of us here are left to sweep up the places in our hearts where she's lived, she is with the bigger part of the Family. And at this reunion, she won't get the award for being the oldest relative present. No! This will be a welcome-home party for the newest kid on the block.

Evelyn Underhill wrote, "Don't lose your head over what perishes."

When Friends Are Not Enough

When I was very young, I was a dare-
devil; I swung out of trees and tested my
aptitude as an aviator by jumping off my
grandfather's chicken coop with an
umbrella. I played ice hockey with
the neighborhood boys and hung on
the back of their motorbikes when my
mother wasn't looking. There were few phys-
ical feats I wouldn't attempt. I believed I could lick the world.

In late grade school, I learned I wasn't so talented at sports stuff
after all. I was one of the last names called when the softball captains
were choosing up sides. The pitcher's ball missed my bat more than
it connected. I couldn't seem to get the eight wheels of my roller
skates going in the same direction. I had lost my confidence. I backed
off. Being poor to mediocre at something was not a good feeling, so
I turned my competitive side to books and word games and spelling
bees and making dollhouses out of matchboxes.

Then one day, at age thirty-five, someone dragged me up a ski
hill. I was sure I couldn't succeed. I would be embarrassed. I was! I
would fail. I did! I was bruised, stiff, and sore, but I loved it. Now, as
often as time and money allow, I head to the slopes!

When we were children, most of us had a rag doll or a teddy
whom we treated ever so tenderly. We had tea parties for dolls—or
for other make-believe friends for whom we baked mud pies and created dandelion and holly berry salads. We caught butterflies and
grasshoppers and woolly worms, fed them, and tried to make them
comfortable. We were the mother-protectors of gerbils and goldfish,
kittens and puppies.

Much later, for many of us, that nurturer-protector translated
into companion, colleague, spouse, neighbor, mother, advocate . . .
and yes, friend. The progression came quite naturally. And for a
period of time, we were caught up in the satisfaction (and exhaustion) of daily tasks—preoccupied with business, housework, child
care, social obligations and endeavors.

But then, something—perhaps something quite unforeseen—
happened. Abruptly, the familiar pattern of our everyday was inter-

rupted: we were rebuffed; feelings of inadequacy swept over us; no longer were we sure we would be "chosen" or "accepted." We felt unqualified, disorganized, overwhelmed by responsibility, and utterly unappreciated. Perhaps a husband was suddenly absent or seemed increasingly unaware or even abusive. A child was pursuing unwholesome relationships; we feared the consequences of his or her lifestyle, but the situation was beyond our daily influence. The pitcher was missing our bat—we couldn't get all our wheels going in the same direction. We were embarrassed. We felt we had failed.

The natural response to this kind of trauma is often to retreat to a very lonely place. There we are imprisoned by fear and disappointment. We find ourselves in a place of total isolation to which we can't invite even the most trustworthy friend. It may be that we can't find the courage or the words to tell our story. Perhaps it isn't ours to tell. Maybe the only friend who can be trusted is the one who doesn't have the life experience to understand. The one who might understand is already overburdened or cannot be trusted to keep the confidence.

As an adult, I have often thought back to what must have been moments of intense loneliness in the life of my mother—a pastor's wife, living hundreds of miles from her family, in a place where her friends were also members of the church congregation. To whom could she go when she felt hurt or abused, emotionally deserted by her husband, or rebuffed by some insensitive church member? The risk of sharing her pain was too great.

When I was a teenager, our home was a refuge for many missionaries and pastors and their families. These were people who, for long periods of time, were starved for intimate companionship, were culturally and intellectually estranged. I remember the emotional relief on their faces as they found in my parents a sincere empathy for their joys and sorrows.

As a wife and mother, I have found myself in an excruciatingly silent zone between a child and her father—desperately trying to maintain the delicate balance of trust and integrity with both husband and child, yet meet the needs of both. I knew that there was not a soul with whom I could share my frustration without betraying a sacred trust.

It is at times like these we say to ourselves, "Okay, grab hold here. Snap out of it! Stop feeling sorry for yourself. Do something positive. Find someone who needs you and redirect your energies."

We get out the emotional broom and industriously begin sweeping the hurts beneath the carpet. We search out the little child in us who found comfort and delight in the care of the teddy bear or box turtle. We seek solace in a kind act or a note of encouragement to another hurting soul. But the teddy lies forlornly limp in our arms, and we can find only emptiness where once there was a wellspring of hope to share.

Suddenly, we are seized by the terrible realization that we once looked at people—people like this person we have now become—with a self-righteous eye. Though at the time, we were unaware of our superior attitudes, we blush with shame to realize how we judged those hurting souls. We had all the answers. We could handle it.

But that was before . . .

> . . . the announcement of a spouse's incurable illness
> . . . a son's alternative lifestyle became a destructive force in his parents' once secure relationship
> . . . the failure of a business into which we had poured our lifeblood and earthly resources
> . . . we discovered a letter, filled with filthy language, revealing a young daughter's portentous obsession with undesirable people
> . . . the burden of caring for aging parents drove a wedge into family relationships
> . . . a son's life, full of promise, was threatened by severe chemical imbalance and depression
> . . . the ravaging exposure of a husband's unfaithfulness
> . . . a child was stolen away from us by satanic forces
> . . . health problems forced us to face our own mortality

Between the four families, Gloria, Sue, Peg, and I have lived some of these agonizing, lonely moments. To our surprise, we found that even the extraordinary friendships we share weren't enough to carry us through the storm. God allowed us to experience the devastation of our private hells so that we could learn to draw upon the resources of a Sovereign God—One who unreservedly offers us not solutions, not answers, not happy-ever-after endings, but His glad welcome—the assurance of His presence with us. His friendship.

Ephesians 3:12 is our warranty: "We can come fearlessly right into God's presence, assured of his glad welcome when we come with Christ and trust in him" (TLB). He never misses our bat; we never need be embarrassed. To me, "glad welcome" sounds a lot like understanding, acceptance, compassion! It also sounds a lot like "friend."

Assured of His glad welcome, we can take our places in a world full of people like ourselves—people who are "out on the edge," who don't know where to turn, who never in a million years expected to find themselves in their present circumstances—people for whom there are no answers but Jesus Christ—and we can do it joyfully!

There are moments in the harsh bleakness of Winter that would be unbearable if there were not, tucked deep within its bosom, the promise of Spring. But Spring always comes. Dark moments in the life and heart of a mother or wife are mitigated only in the light of God's sovereignty—and we can know that, though our personal journey may end before we see the blossoms of Spring, the rain always comes again. The desert has its edge, and in God's timing, the darkness will give way to light.

When We Grow Old

Bob was just finishing college and ready to leave for seminary when we married. He teasingly said he needed a wife who could talk to "anyone, anywhere, on any subject." I jokingly replied that it didn't matter if I knew anything about the subject at hand. I could talk on it anyway! He said that if I married him and became a preacher's wife, it would be like living in a goldfish bowl. I said I didn't have anything to hide and I would love the attention. He told people I was so small when we married I had to stand on a box to reach the sink. That's almost true! Not only was I small in physical stature, I was small in experience too. We told people we "grew ourselves up together." In the thirty-four years we were married, our lives took many turns—from pastoring to managing a large music business, juggling his speaking and writing schedule, to raising five children and building a large home.

Peggy

They say that people who live together for a long time and are very close begin to think, act, talk, walk, and even look alike. We had arrived at the place in life where it took both of us to finish a story.

During the last weeks of Bob's life, I sat by his bed and wrote him a letter. When he was awake, I would read portions of it aloud.

My Dear Bob,

I really meant to save some of these things to tell you later, when we were old, perhaps while we walked the beach together with the sun beaming down on leathery brown skin and stiff, sore limbs. I pictured us with slouch hats covering our gray heads as our eyes strained to look once more for a perfect seashell. I realize as I sit here watching you struggle to breathe that we probably won't be growing old together. What a shame. You would be the most darling little old man! Something tells me I need to make sure this very night, this very hour, you know that I know what a treasure our life together has been. As I watch you wince in pain, I pray it's almost time for more morphine. You begin to stir and awaken and smile up at me as I stand over your bed and fluff your pillow. I bathe your face to keep the fever down. I decide it's time to let you know some things.

For instance, did you know there have been times I've wondered if we've suffered from loving each other too much? Your loving me has been the best part—the very essence and core of my life. Any goodness I possess is because you loved me and said so. Not only do I love you, my darling, I really, really like you! You will think this is crazy, but I love that little touch of mystery you have about you. It's as if you have kept a little something of yourself to yourself all these years. I have found that exciting about you. Even challenging. I like your warped sense of humor, your gentle ways, your timid approach, your egotistical non-ego—whatever that means. You always made me feel I was the most important person in the room. In your life!

Do you remember once we attended a wedding where the bride and groom lit candles and then together, lit a unity candle, then blew out their individual ones? You turned to me and said, "I don't like that candle business. I don't believe God wants us to blow each other out when we become one. Marriage shouldn't extinguish us. It should make us more of who and what we are." Through the years, you pretty much lived that out in our life together. You had the ability to hold me close and then to let me go—free to be and to grow at my own pace. That was very "tricky" of you because it made me love you more.

As I think back over our years, I can't help but wonder: *Where did they go? Why were we so busy?* Even our conversations were in bits and snatches. There were children to keep and yards to mow, church services to attend and work to do. Ball games and PTA. Books to write. Speaking engagements. Gardens to grow and vacations to take.

In the midst of our busyness, you were smart enough to make sure we had *our time* together. Time to dream and to plan. There were sketches and plans drawn on paper napkins at some corner table in a restaurant. We planned beach houses we would share with family and friends and a writer's cottage in the woods. We talked about trips to Nantucket and excursions to Europe. Those were things we dreamed we would do, but in reality you made sure we took trips together where there was time alone to make love without interruption of children. Afterwards there was time for long walks, leisurely dinners, and conversations about our dreams and plans and children and friends. I can't remember if I told you how important those getaways were to me. They were like visiting some great, holy cathedral and hearing the organ raise its voice in praise to God. Those small private times with you are still, after all these years, saving my life! Did I remember to thank you for all you've meant to my life? For all you have taught me?

For being strong when I was weak.
For teaching me to let go of small, petty hurts.
For reminding me to save up for the big stuff of life.
For not getting so caught up in the crisis of life that I missed life!

Eleven years have passed. Recently I wrote this postscript:

Most of the time since you went away, I've been strong and resilient. You would be proud! I don't give up or give in easily. Some days I miss you so badly I could just die! Only on rainy days, sunny days, birthdays, holidays, normal days, and abnormal days. I miss your skinny body, your shaky hands, that crooked little finger, the cowlick you hated so, your old tweed jacket, your slouch rain hat, your sense of humor, your love notes scratched on the grocery list and written on the mirror, and your lazy lips. Especially on mine! I even miss all those millions of little pieces of paper with book notes scratched on them that I was forbidden to throw away.

The truth is *I am plain old lonesome to see you!* Lonely for our life together. I miss our house, our sitting room overlooking the water, our old bedroom, our covers. I miss *ourselves.* Where did *we* go? When I get this lonely, I could scream! Sometimes I do. There are times I feel as if you've gone and left me with a lot of strangers whose faces I recognize.

When you went away, you took a part of me with you. When I see you again someday . . . and I will . . . I will claim that part of myself again and I will recognize it, because that part of me is you. Sometimes when I look in the mirror for *me,* I see *us!*

Once Peg jokingly said, "I'd like to go to my own funeral so I could hear what people said about me, to find out if they liked me and thought me worthwhile!"

Good friends don't wait to say they love each other. If there is something you've meant to tell your friend or loved one or mate … Don't wait!

A Nun's Prayer

Lord, thou knowest better than I know myself that I am growing older, and will someday be old.

Keep me from getting talkative, and particularly from the fatal habit of thinking I must say something on every subject and on every occasion.

Release me from craving to try to straighten out everybody's affairs.

Keep my mind free from the recital of endless details . . . give me wings to get to the point.

I ask for grace enough to listen to the tales of others' pains. Help me to endure them with patience.

But seal my lips on my own aches and pains . . . they are increasing and my love of rehearsing them is becoming sweeter as the years go by.

Teach me the glorious lesson that occasionally it is possible that I may be mistaken.

Keep me reasonably sweet; I do not want to be a saint . . . some of them are so hard to live with . . . but a sour old woman is one of the crowning works of the devil.

Make me thoughtful, but not moody; helpful, but not bossy. With my vast store of wisdom, it seems a pity not to use it all . . . but thou knowest, Lord, that I want a few friends at the end.

by a Mother Superior,
who wishes to remain anonymous

That's What Girlfriends Are For!

In my next life, I'm going to have a husband who will listen to me with compassion. When I am sad or hurting or out-of-sorts, he won't have advice or a fix-it; there will be no put-down, no jokes, no sarcasm. After we finish an honest discussion, each having expressed his or her feelings— which may include raised voices, crying, argument, or even evidence of bitter disappointment—I will still feel cherished, as will he.

I am married to a man who has many wonderful qualities of character and a stellar collection of imperfections that makes him fascinating. (Perfection is, after all, rather boring.) I do not like every aspect of his personality, but I find the sum total of them irresistible. However, if I had a magic genie, my one wish would be that he would always respond to my fears and problems and complaints—yes, even the foolish, unfounded, unintelligible, emotional, overdramatized (female-ish) ones—with simple kindness and compassion.

Most likely, I will unremittingly pursue my perfectly female, "woman-from-Venus" dream, and he will continue to react in his thoroughly male, "man-from-Mars" pattern. (The incompatibility issue is something I am surely going to put on my list of questions to ask the Almighty when I meet Him face-to-face!) Meanwhile, in exasperated reaction to this continuing—I hope, not *eternal*—dilemma, I have come to understand why girlfriends are so important.

A husband—or any man, I suppose—may be an extraordinary human being and a best friend, but it is a very unusual man who can match some of the high standards of a really close girlfriend! I ask you ... With whom but a girlfriend can you

... be shamelessly silly?

... reason in a totally illogical manner, without fear of judgment?

... blubber with guaranteed consolation?

... change your mind without explanation?

... recite endless details with no point?

... be absolutely honest about how much you spent for your
   clothes?

... review your husband's annoying habits with laughter?

... or rely on unqualified sympathy for an overweight body, an
   overdue period, or an overbearing mother-in-law?

With how many husbands is a wife free to

... stop and ask for directions?

... serve (or eat) a meal at *her* convenience?

... enter the kitchen without hearing a request for service?

... tidy the house *before* she goes to bed?

... admit she doesn't know (or care) which acronym relates to
   football—AFL or AF of L?

... let down her hair and her defenses at the same time?

One thing I can't do freely with my husband is to shop. However, I have rarely had a girlfriend with whom I haven't shared some sort of memorable shopping experience.

Once Peg and I spent the better part of an afternoon trying on *haute couture* clothing, priced way beyond what we could sneak onto a credit account without arousing the unrighteous ire of our spouses.

The clerks called us "dahling" as they zipped us in and out of glamorous to gaudy outfits, complete with all the proper accessories, assuring us that the results were "just adorable." When we were left alone in our dressing room, we were bent double with laughter, mocking their phony accents and strutting, resplendent and peacockish, in our borrowed finery. Peg's sister, Bo, who witnessed the entire charade, declared that shopping with us was like spending the afternoon with Lucy Ricardo and Ethyl Mertz.

We can't remember an occasion with our husbands when we were so irrepressibly overcome with laughter. Of course, they heard the story repeated many times, and though we were nearly always prostrate on the floor with hilarity at the retelling, they were only mildly amused. I guess you had to be there. They, of course, were thankful they weren't!

There are bumps and snags and hurts in life that shopping trips can't cure. There were years when Peg was sitting in a hospital room with no time to lunch and shop and laugh. In recent years, there has been little time or money for either of us to spend on frivolous joys.

In all of our lives, there are nightmarish moments when our cries are unheard, unheeded, or misunderstood by everyone but another wife or mother.

Persons of the other gender, beloved as they may be, simply do not always speak our language. Their view of reality, though logical and reasonable, reflects a different sense of it than is familiar to women. Pretending that all things are equal and that our perspectives are in harmony—because we are in love or because we are married or just because we desperately want togetherness—covertly undermines our best intentions and often results in hurt, even irreparable damage, to both parties and the relationship.

Volumes have been researched and published on the justifiable differences. The problem dates back to the Garden of Eden. Again, the answer emanates from the wisdom of the Master Gardener who foresaw the gender communication chasm created by the Fall. He provided the models (Ruth and Naomi, Mary and Elizabeth)—after which women may fashion enduring relationships that allow them to share one another's burdens and delights, learn from one another, encourage each other, and together, celebrate their faith.

Knowing that the Sovereign of the universe is vitally interested in the tense moments of my marriage or in the frustration of a casual conversation gone awry is comforting, but even more comforting is the knowing that, beyond each disappointment, is a tangible empathy, an audible wisdom, a visceral joy that He has created for my encouragement and pleasure—I call it *girlfriends*.

Maintenance Tips for a Friendship Garden

Friendship isn't a fifty-fifty proposition. What if you can only afford a fifty-cent greeting card and your friend can afford a fifty-dollar present? *Take the present!* When Dana Buchanan was little, she asked her dad what it meant when he said, "Uncle Bill is going to 'take us out' to dinner." Her daddy explained that "take us out" meant that Uncle Bill would be paying the bill. "What do you think it would mean," he asked, "if I said, 'We're going to take Uncle Bill and Auntie out to dinner?'" Dana thought a minute and said, "It would still mean that Uncle Bill pays. Uncle Bill always pays." It was true. Sue and Wayne had little money and Uncle Bill was more than generous. Dana and her family tried to come up with inexpensive things that would please Uncle Bill and Auntie. One of their best ideas was a crazy cake. They baked several flavors of cake mixes in various sized pans and cans, and then with five or six colors of icing, and an assortment of sprinkles and candies, created the wildest, most outrageous cake imaginable. Uncle Bill was so pleased, he showed it to the whole neighborhood.

A friend helps heal the hurts. Gloria sent Sue a beautiful Blue Mountain Arts card about sisters to which she added: "Sue, my sister—You once said you were lonely for the sister you didn't have. I hope you feel that lonely spot filling in, like a crayon fills in the space between the outline. At least, I feel you are my sister, and this weekend was a wonder. Love and peace, my friend."

Think of yourself as a PR person when it comes to your friends. We say such nice things about each other that we then have to live up to them. Joy tells people that Sue is funny and creative and classy. She knows Sue's faults and could as easily say that Sue has been known to snap people's heads off, that she's bossy, that she speaks before she thinks, and that her eye makeup is usually halfway down her face. There's only one thing Joy regularly tells about Sue that's not complimentary. She takes every opportunity to say how loudly Sue snores—that once on a plane, Sue not only snored, but drooled too! This is not something a PR person would do, but Joy is forgiven. Of course that gives Sue the freedom to say Joy has been known to pull Windex out of her suitcase and clean the windows in a hotel room and that she carries Lysol in her purse to spray toilet seats. Peg and Gloria have heard it all a million times. They still laugh! What friends!

Best Friends . . .

. . . do not have need of us as much as they have the capacity to enjoy us.

. . . walk alongside on life's journey—do not run ahead or lag behind.

. . . are forgetful of what isn't perfect about us.

. . . grow and change with one another—learn from one another's experiences.

. . . share both the important and insignificant pieces of their lives with the same degree of joy and openness.

. . . instinctively know when to talk and when to be silent . . . well, most of the time!

. . . praise with sincerity, criticize with humility, confront with compassion.

Do we have what it takes to be a best friend? Only intermittently and in varying degrees. We have to keep working at it—it's not easy. But the rewards are extraordinary!

Thank God
for the Promise
of Spring

Though the skies be gray above me,
And I can't see the light of day:
There's a ray breaking through the shadows,
And His smile can't be far away.

Thank God for the promise of Springtime,
Once again my heart will sing:
There's a brand-new day a-dawning,
Thank God for the promise of Spring.

Though the earth seems bleak and barren,
And the seeds lay brown and dead:
Oh, the promise of life throbs within them
And I know Spring is just ahead.

Thank God for the promise of Springtime,
Once again my heart will sing:
There's a brand-new day a-dawning,
Thank God for the promise of Spring.

Gloria Gaither